Seasons Adult Coloring Book

This Beautiful Seasons book belongs to:

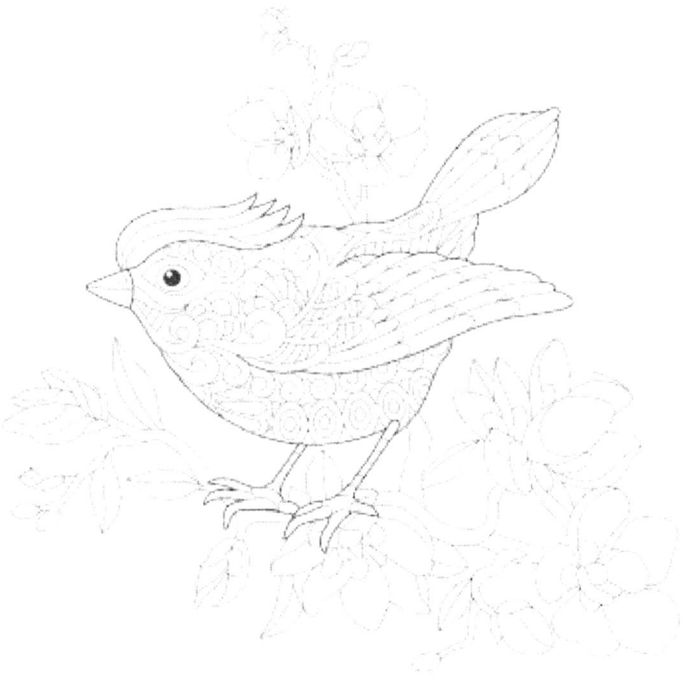

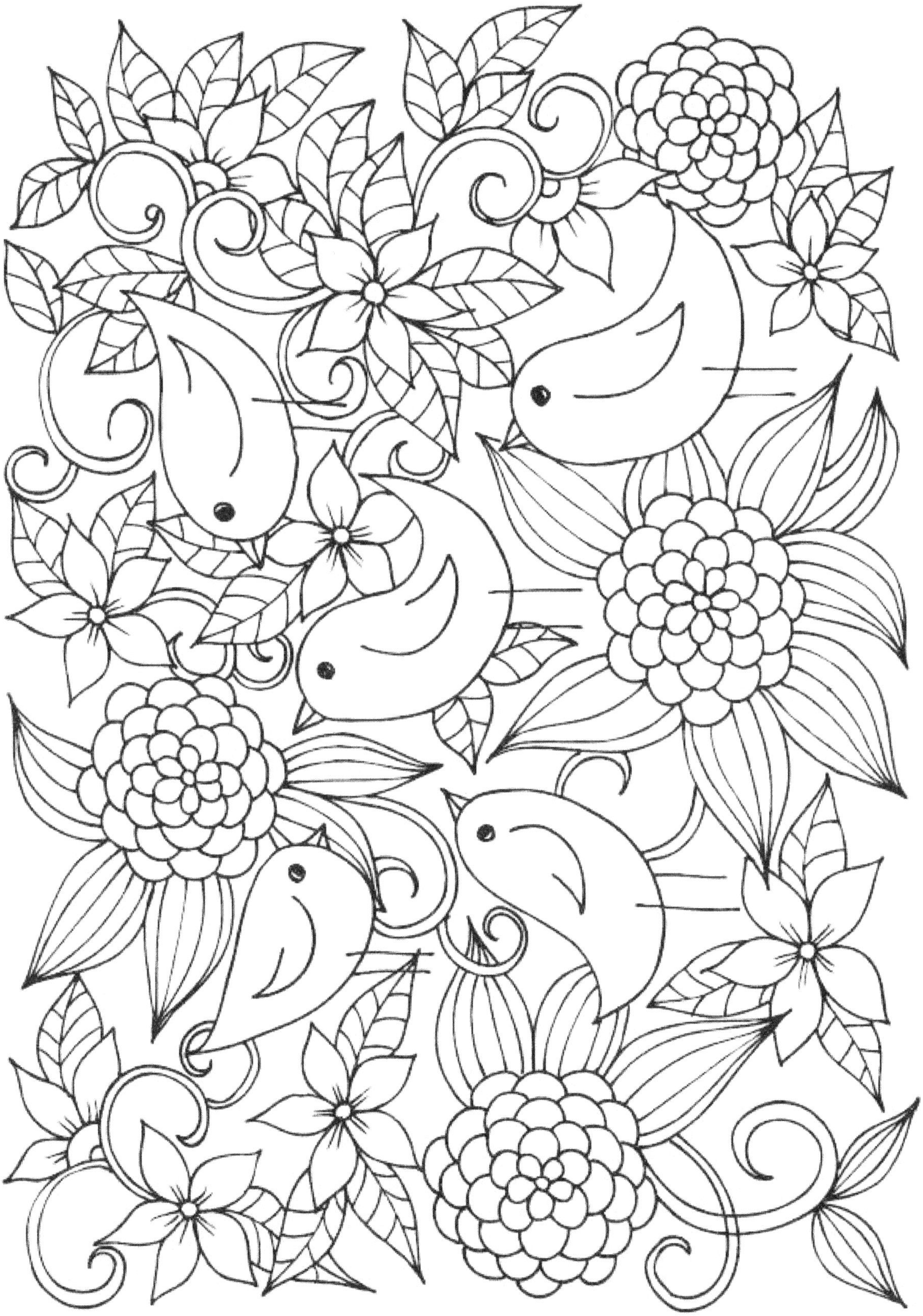

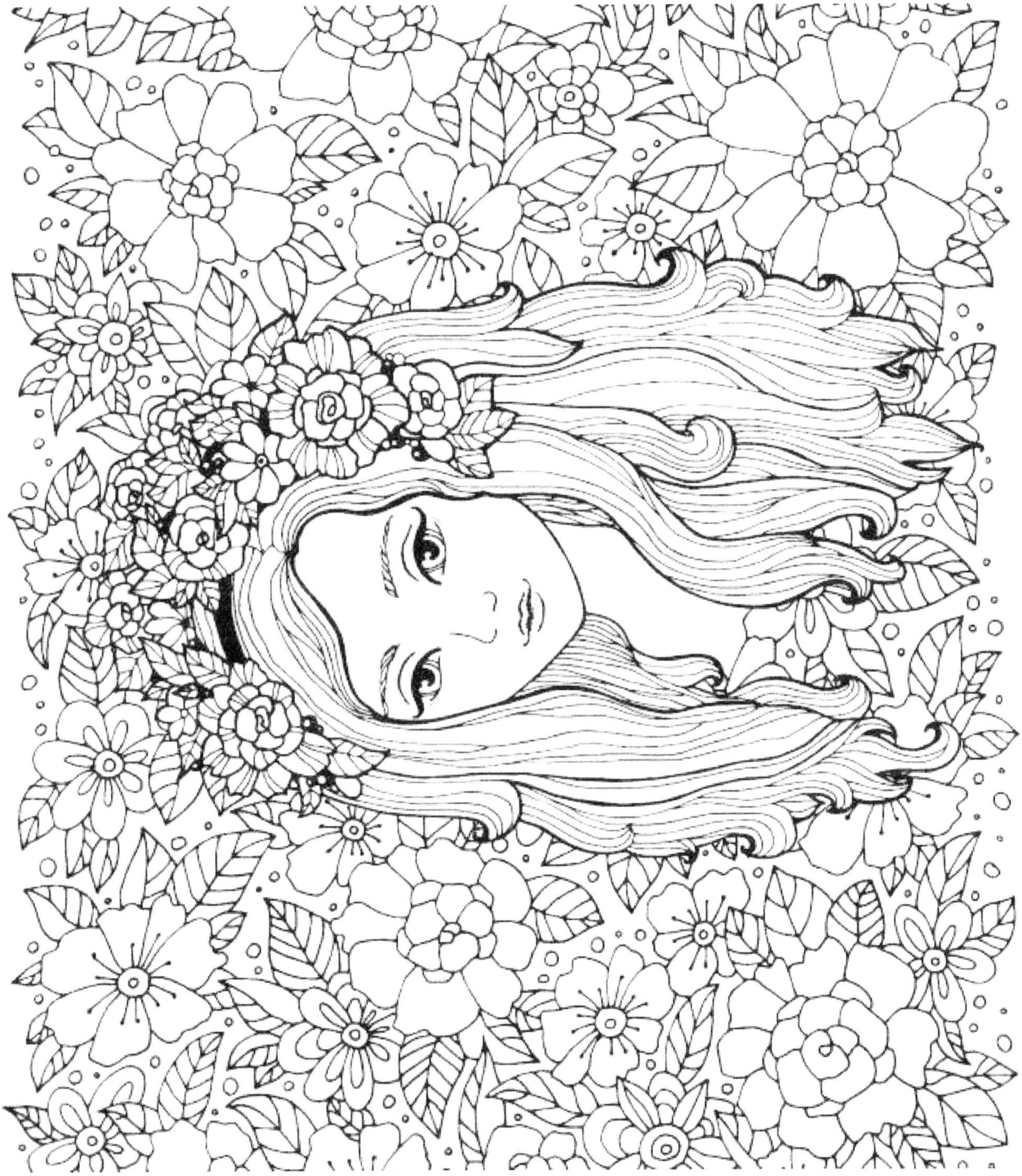

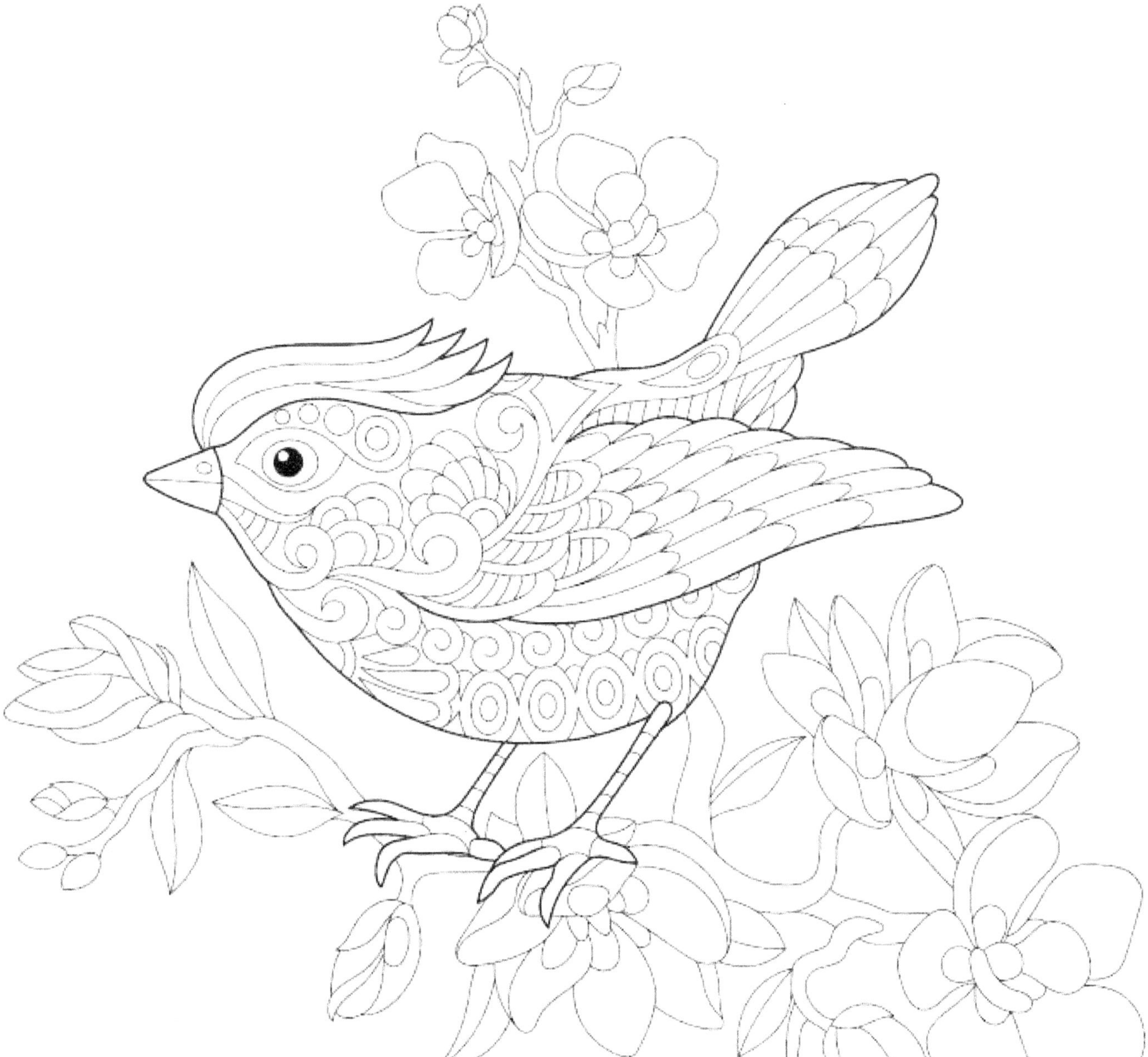

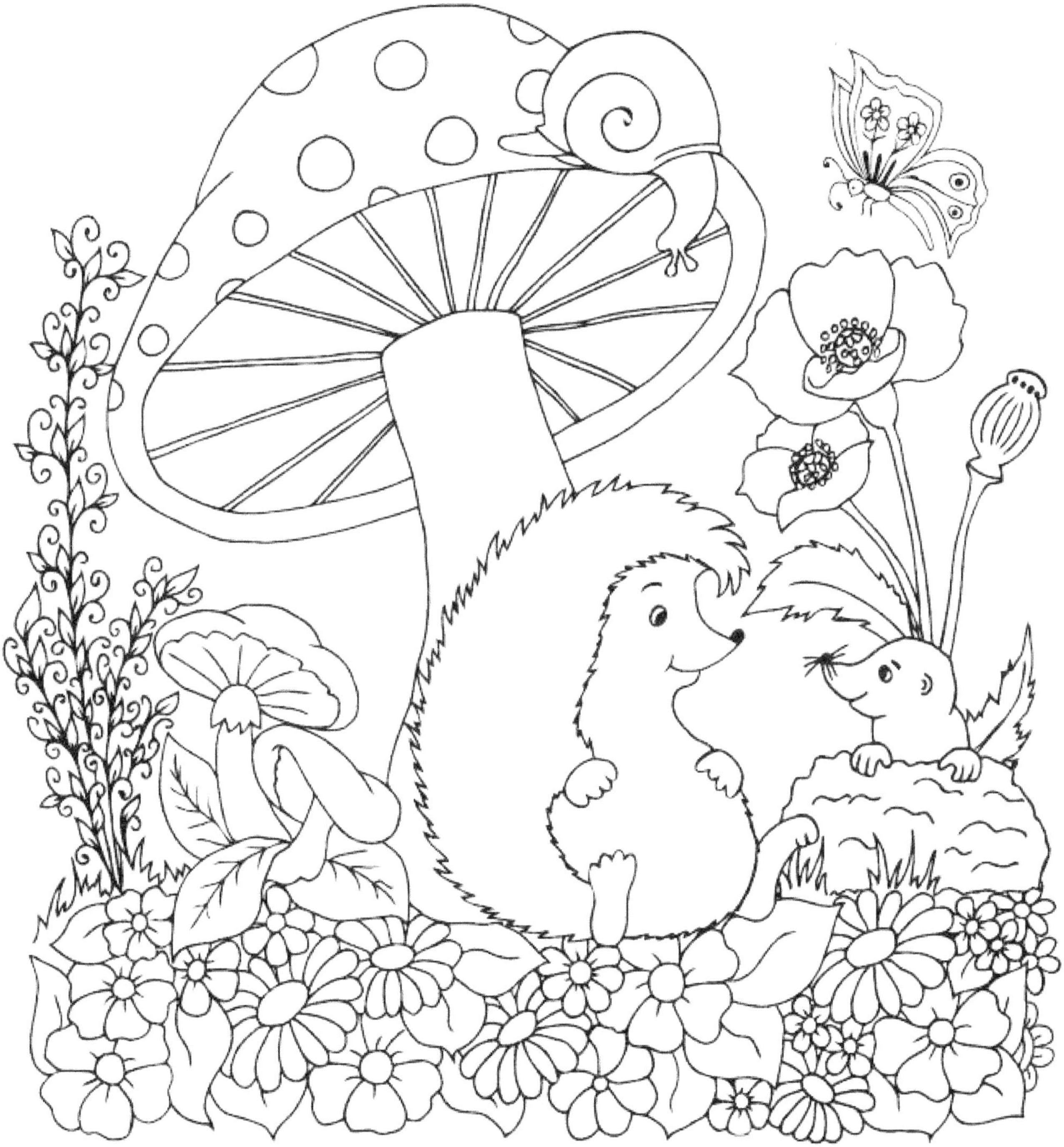

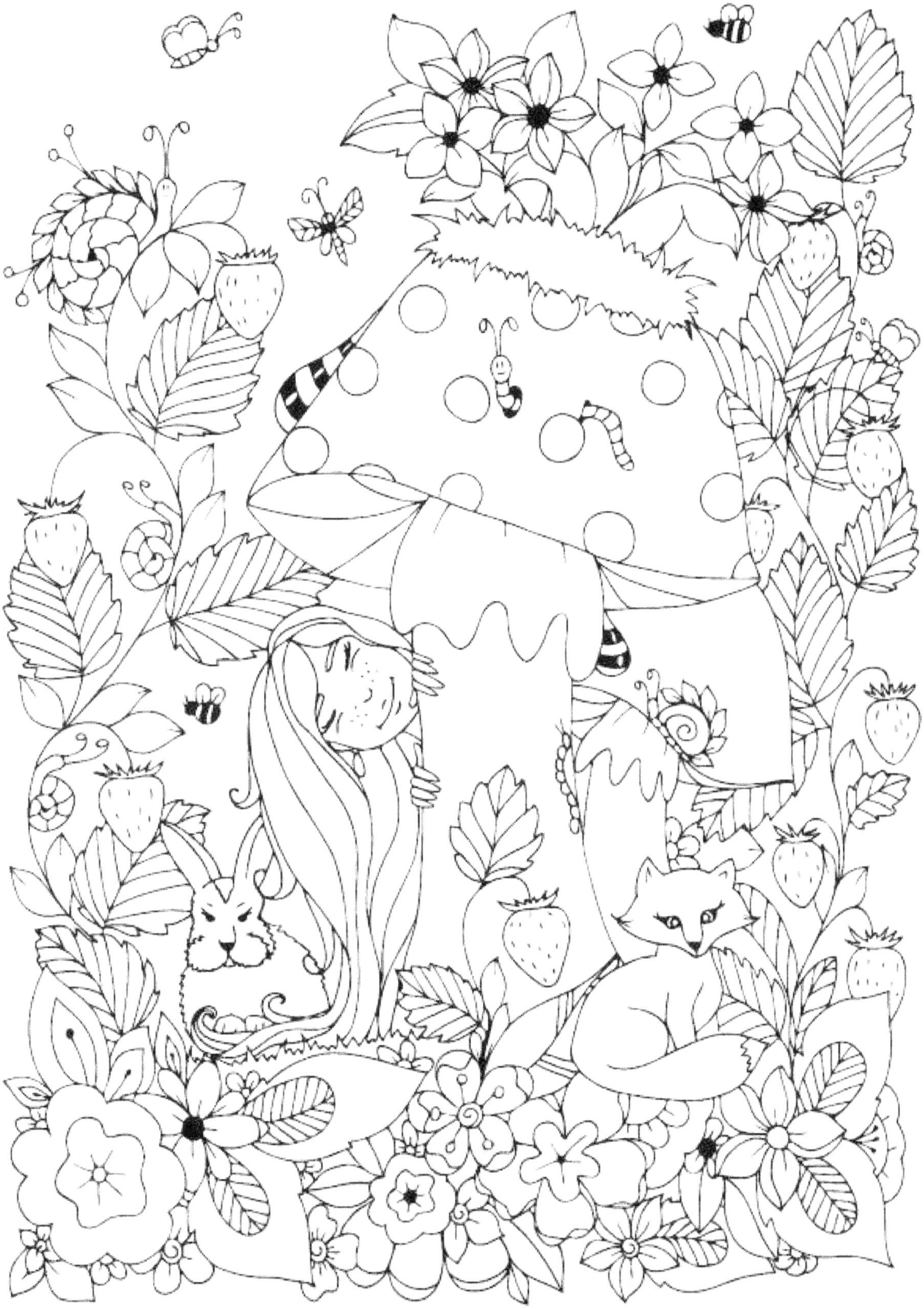

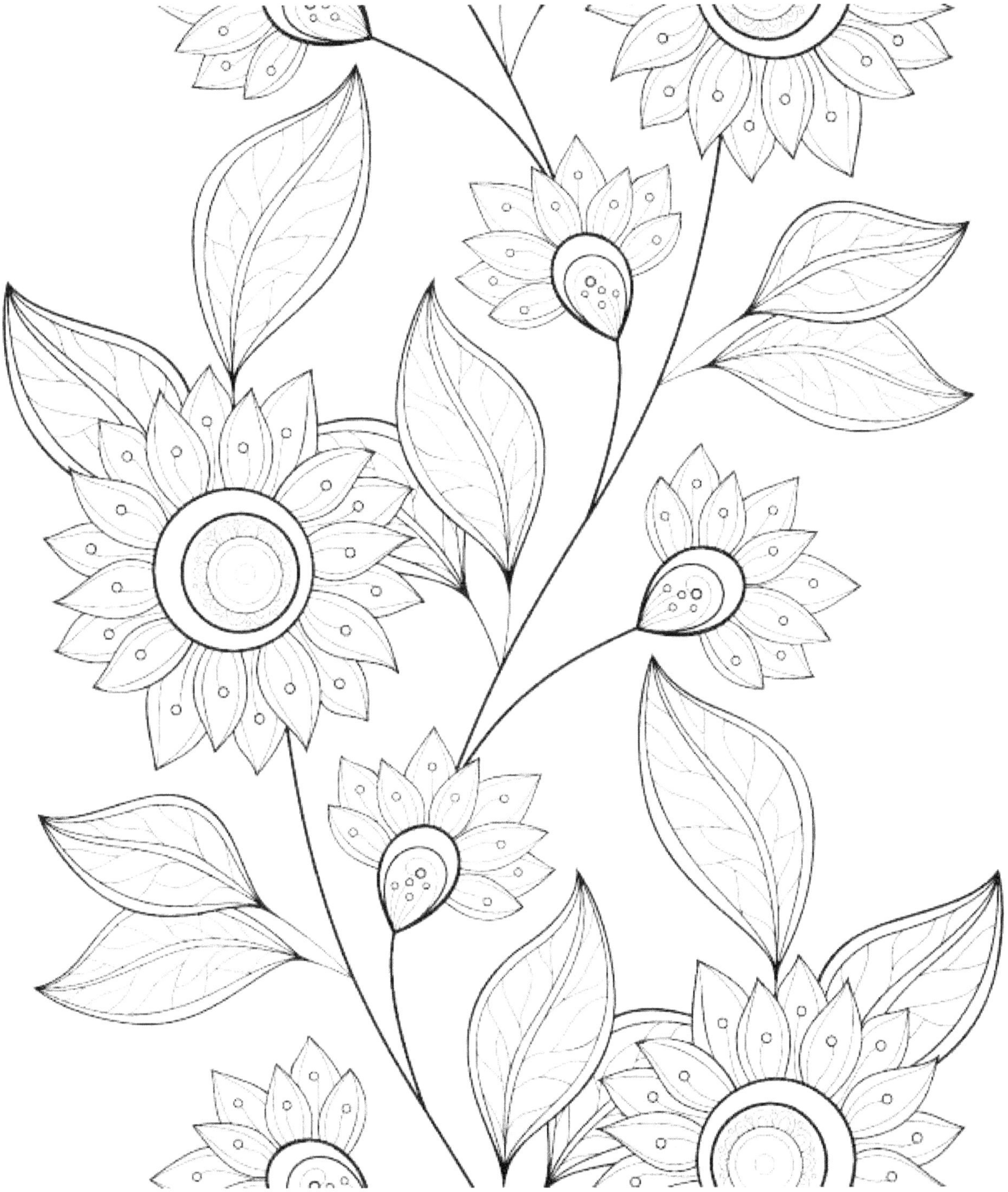

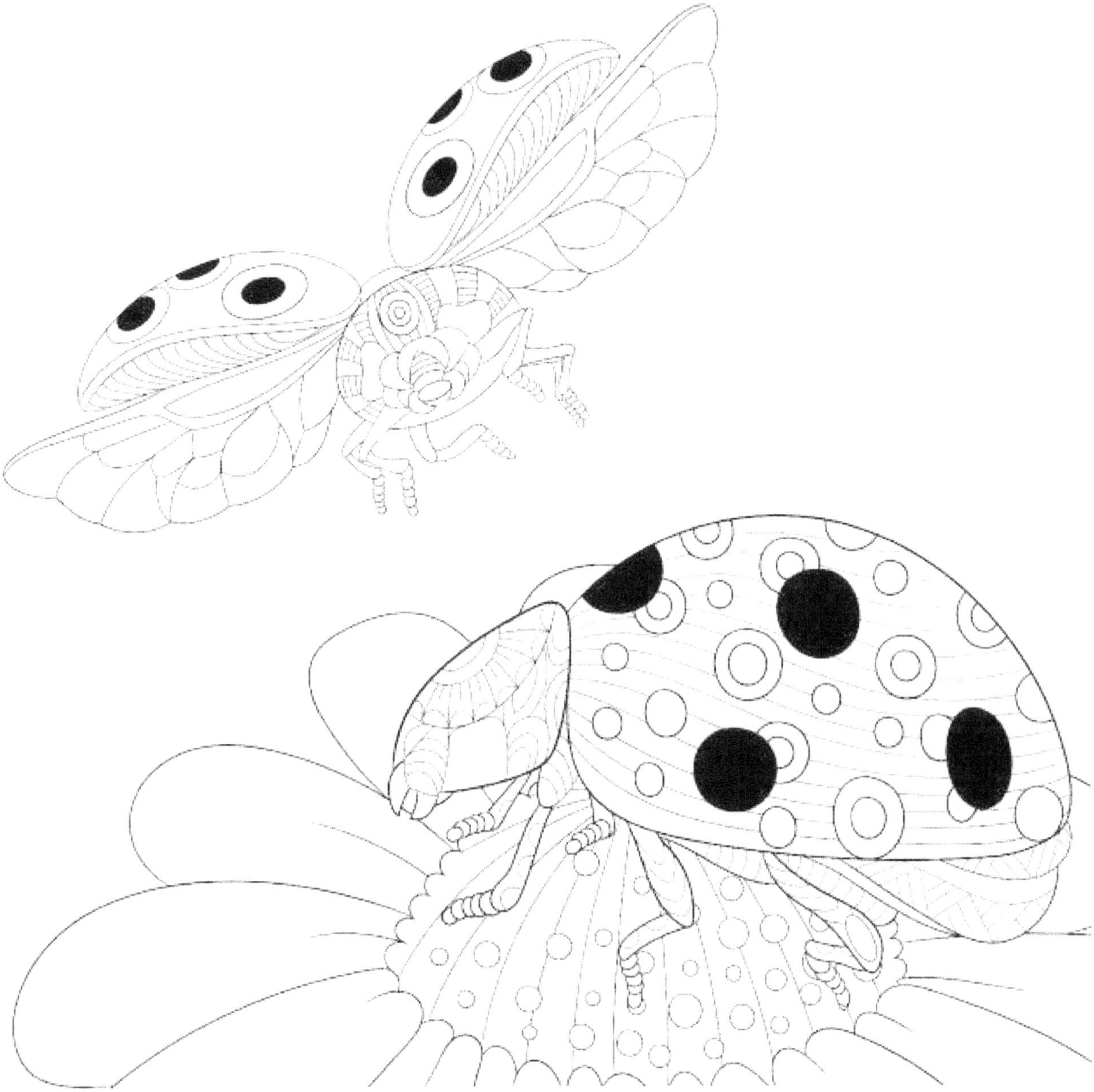

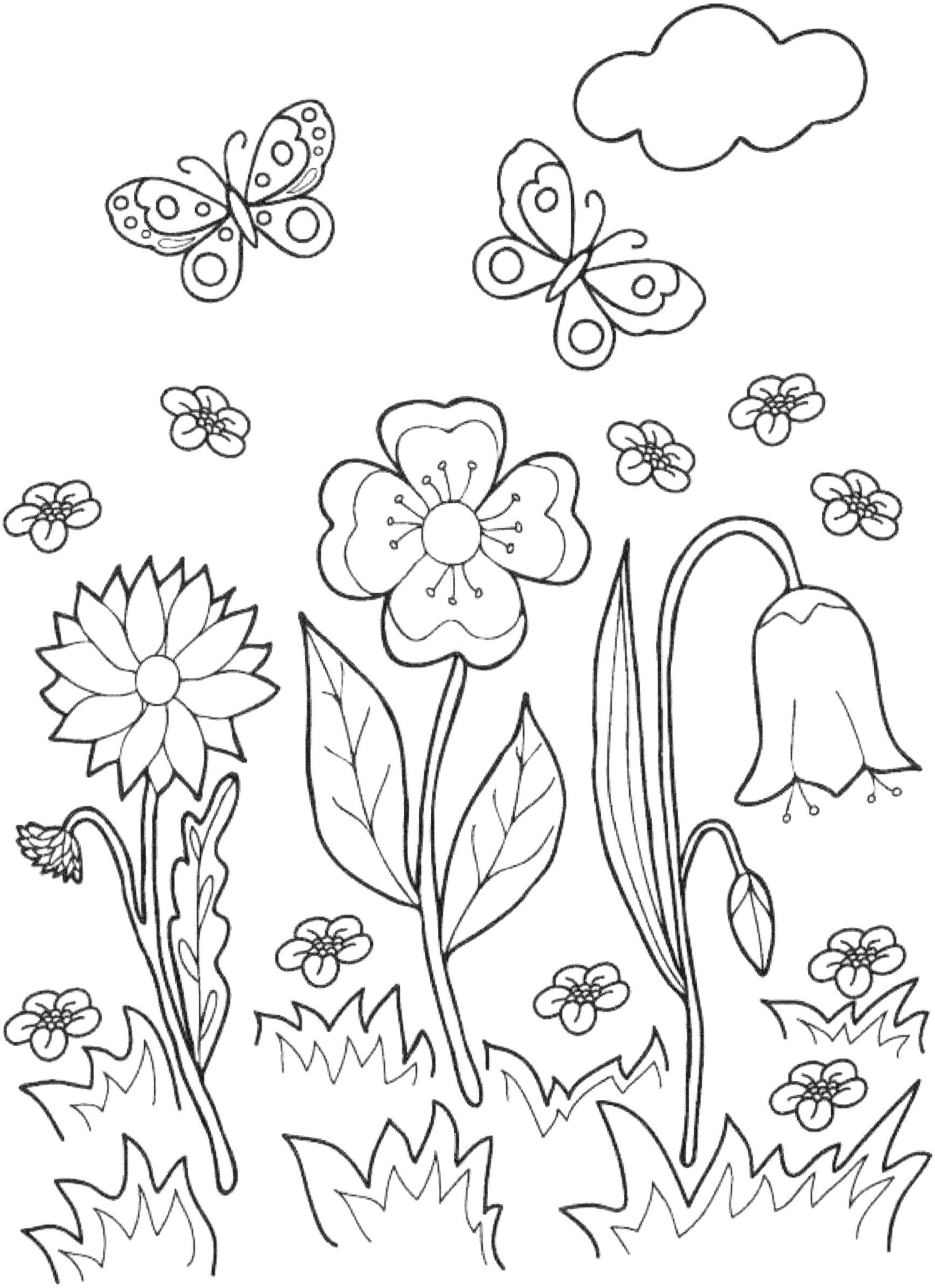

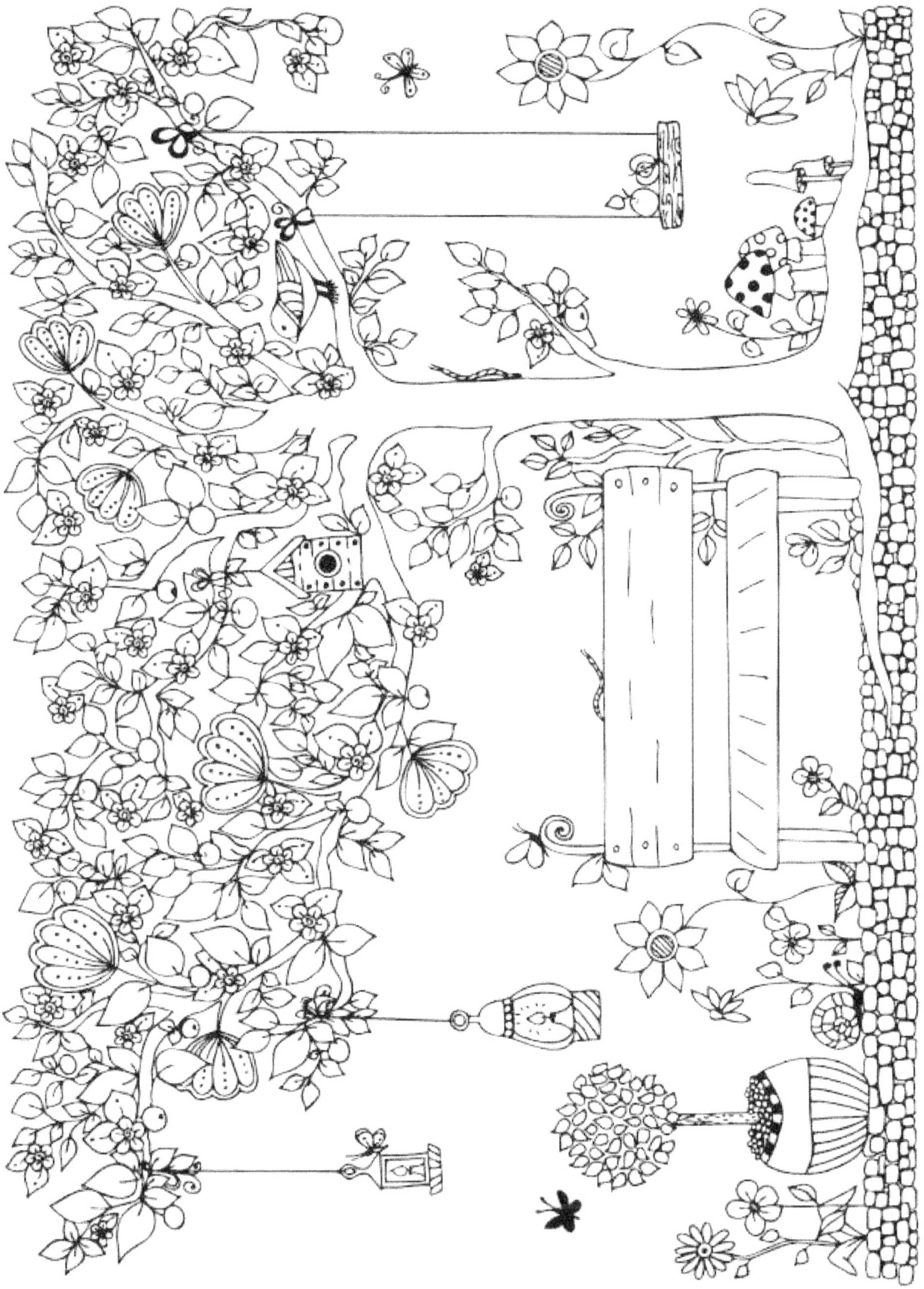

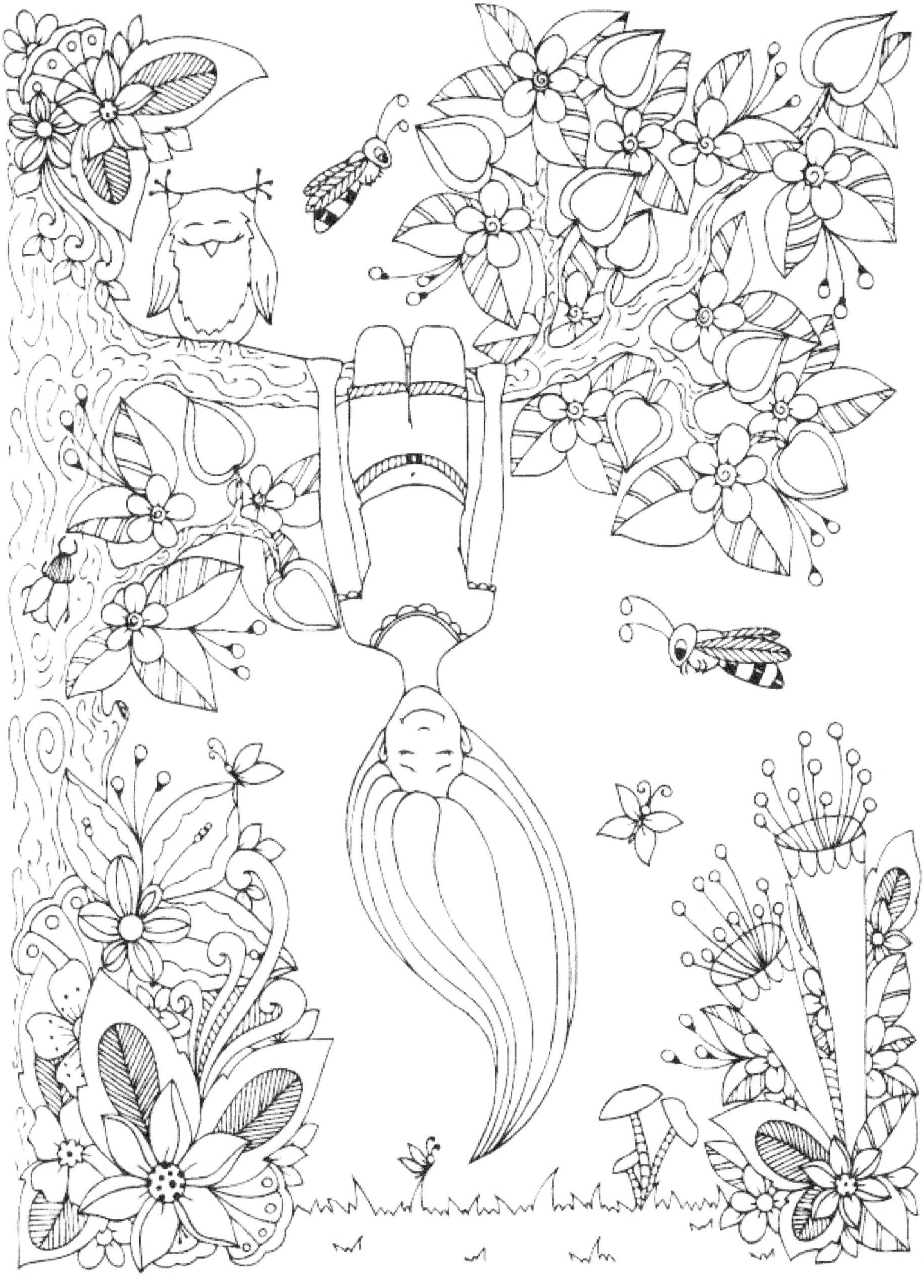

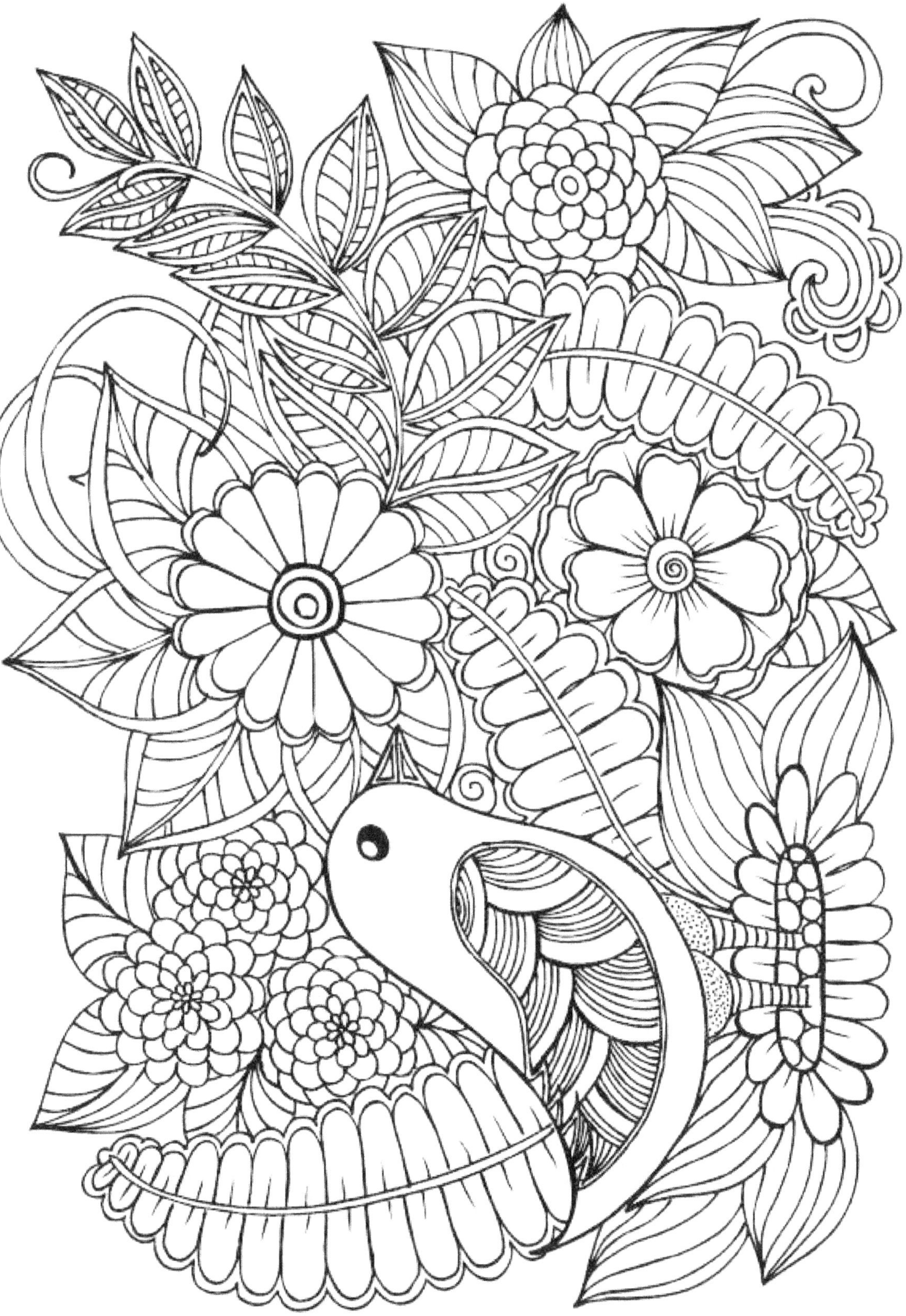

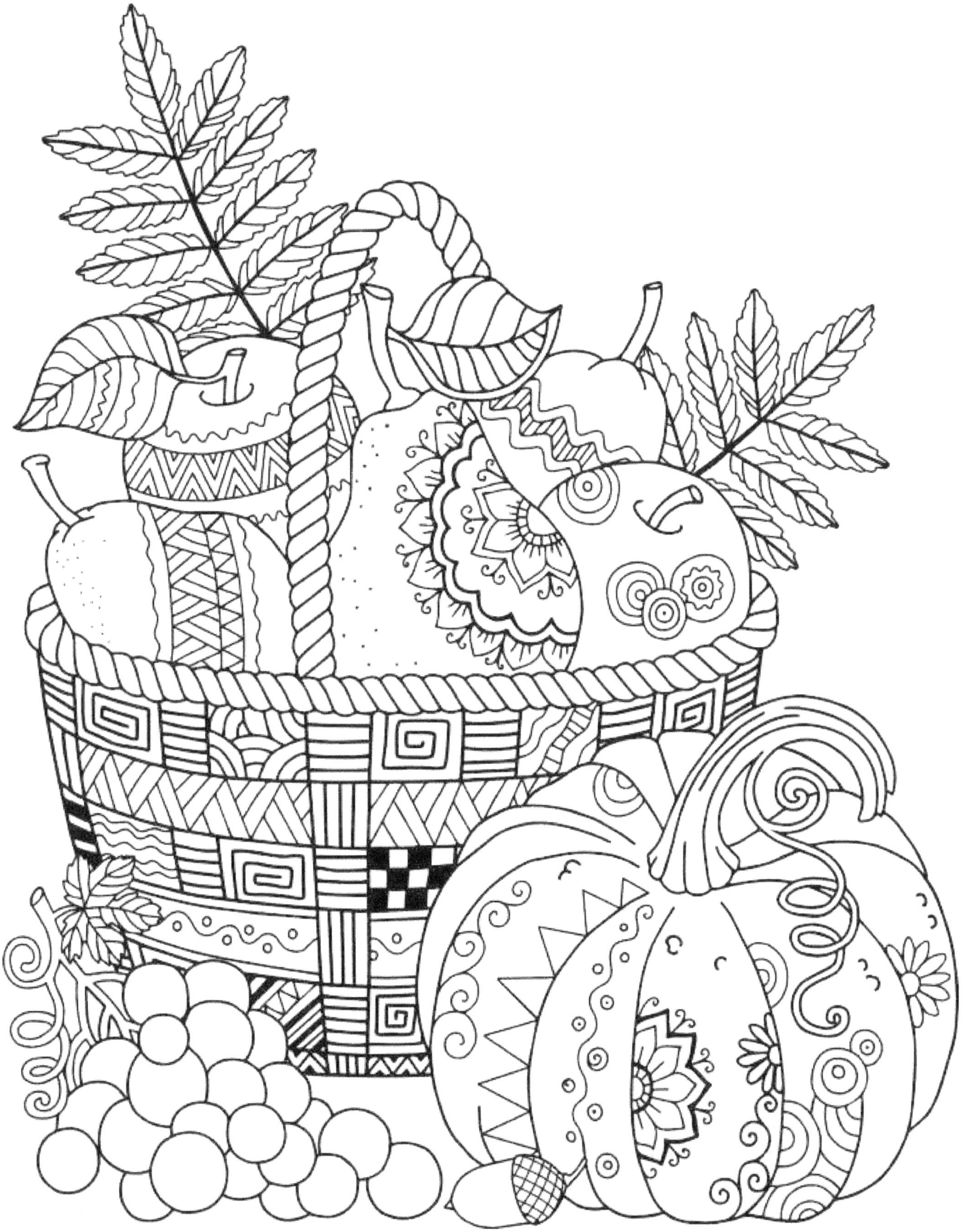

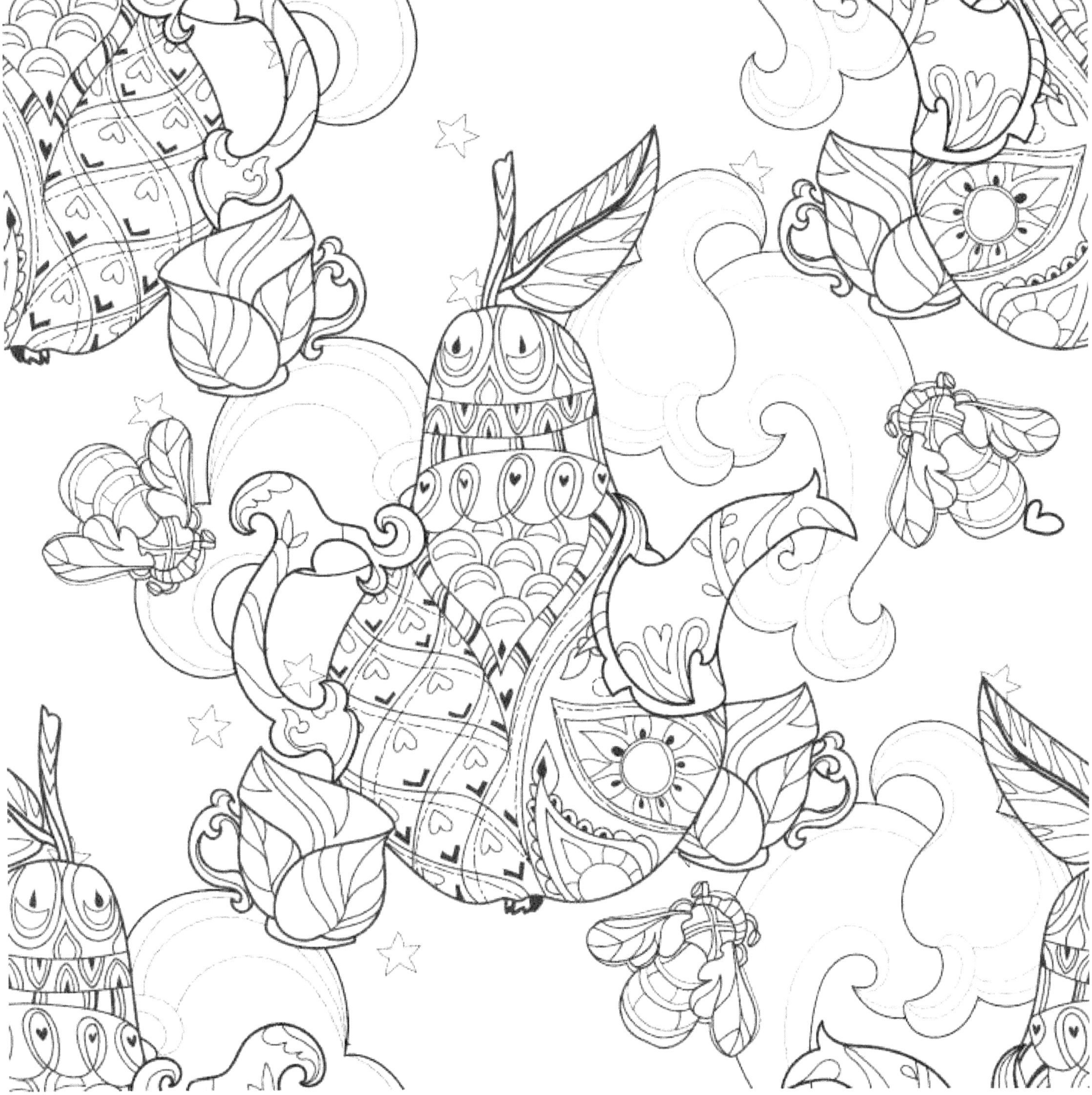

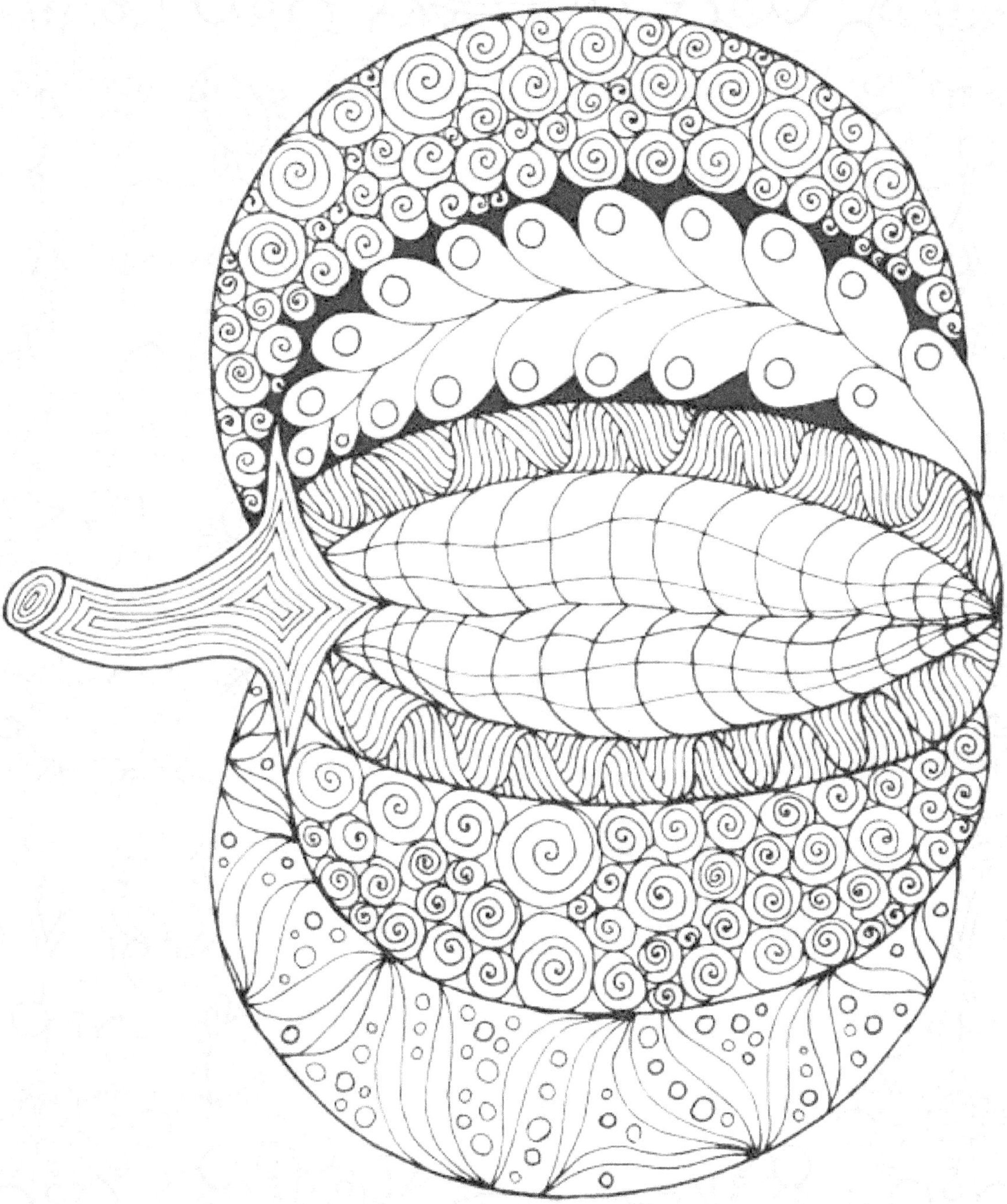

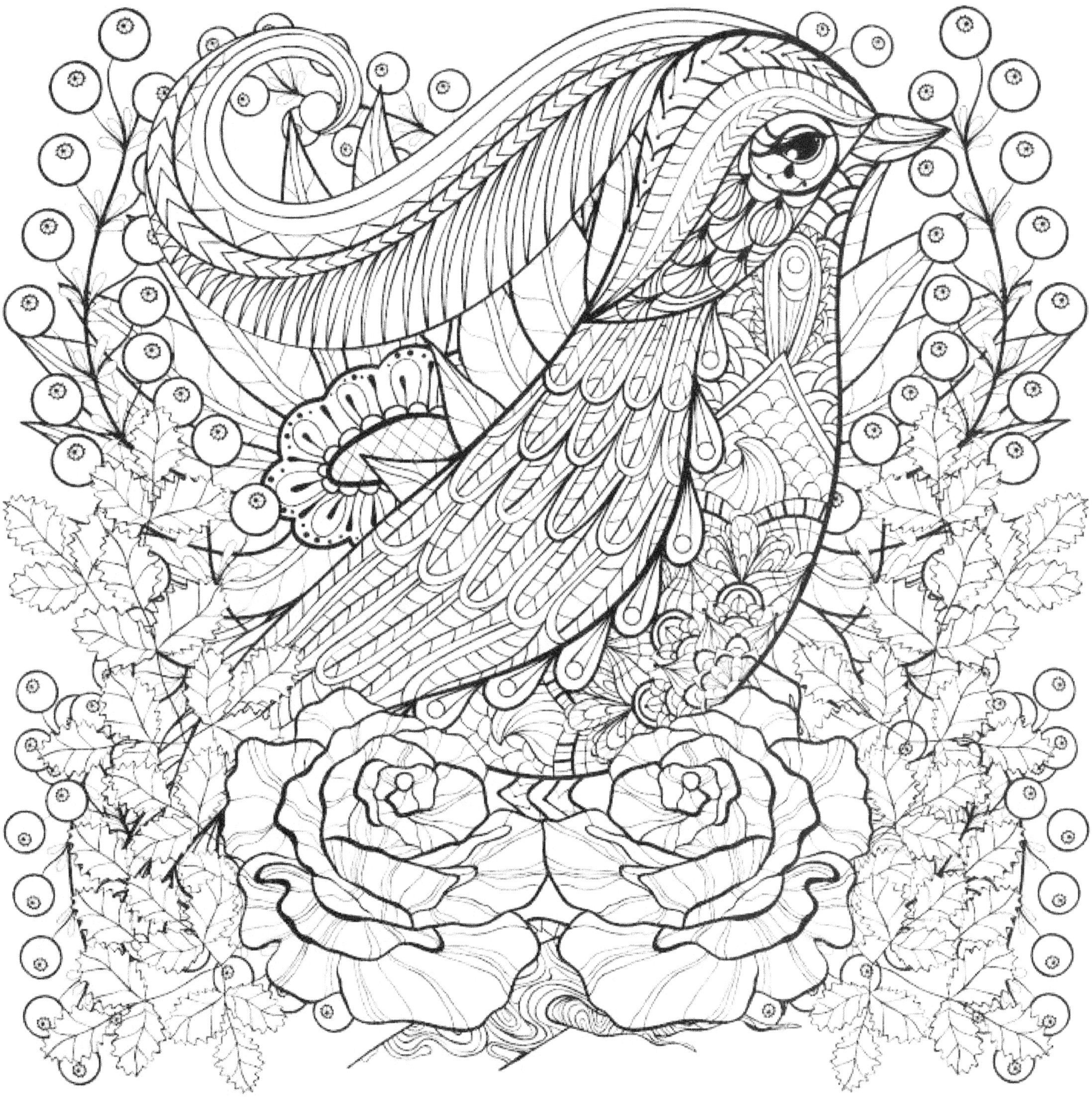

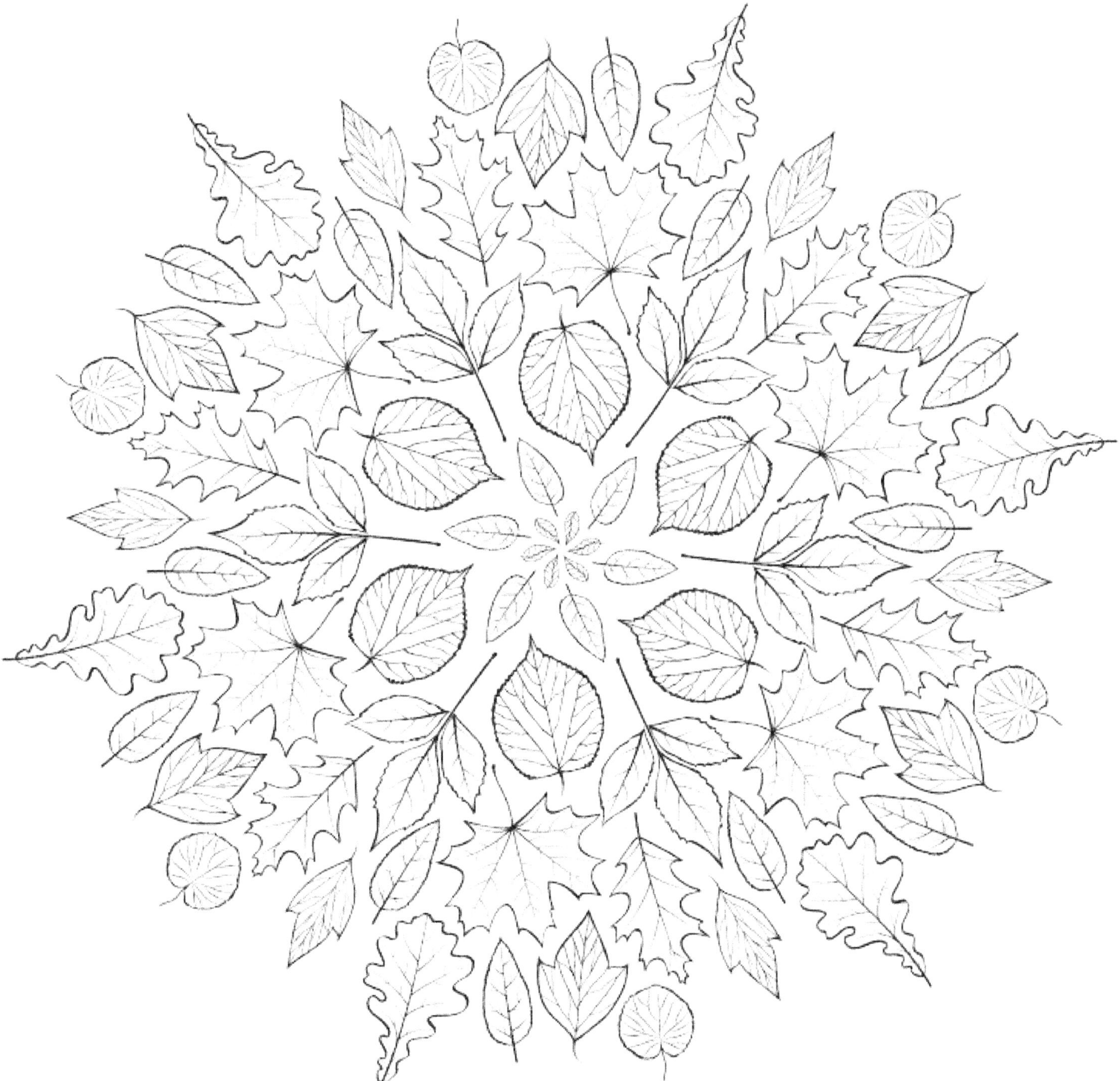

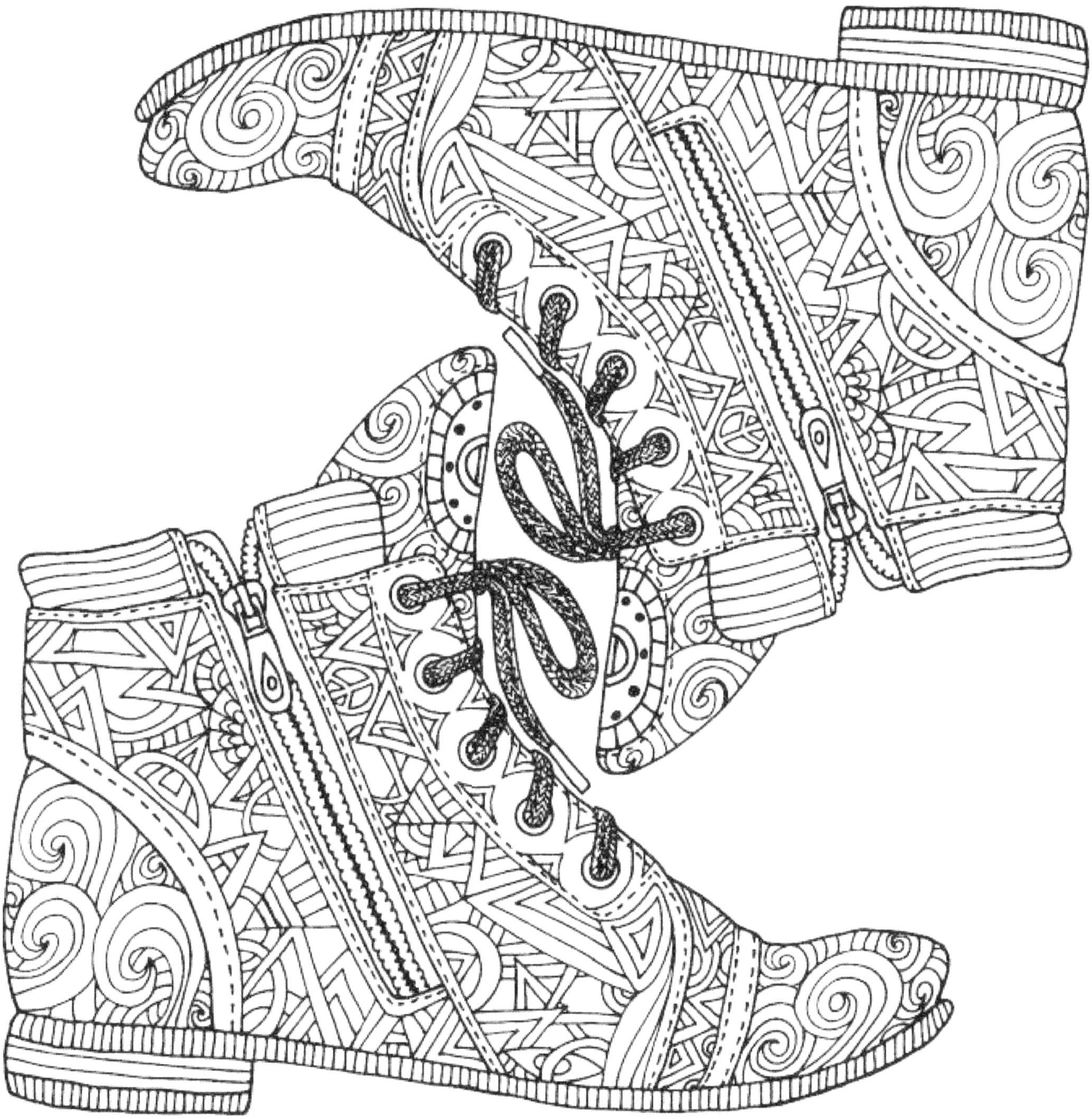

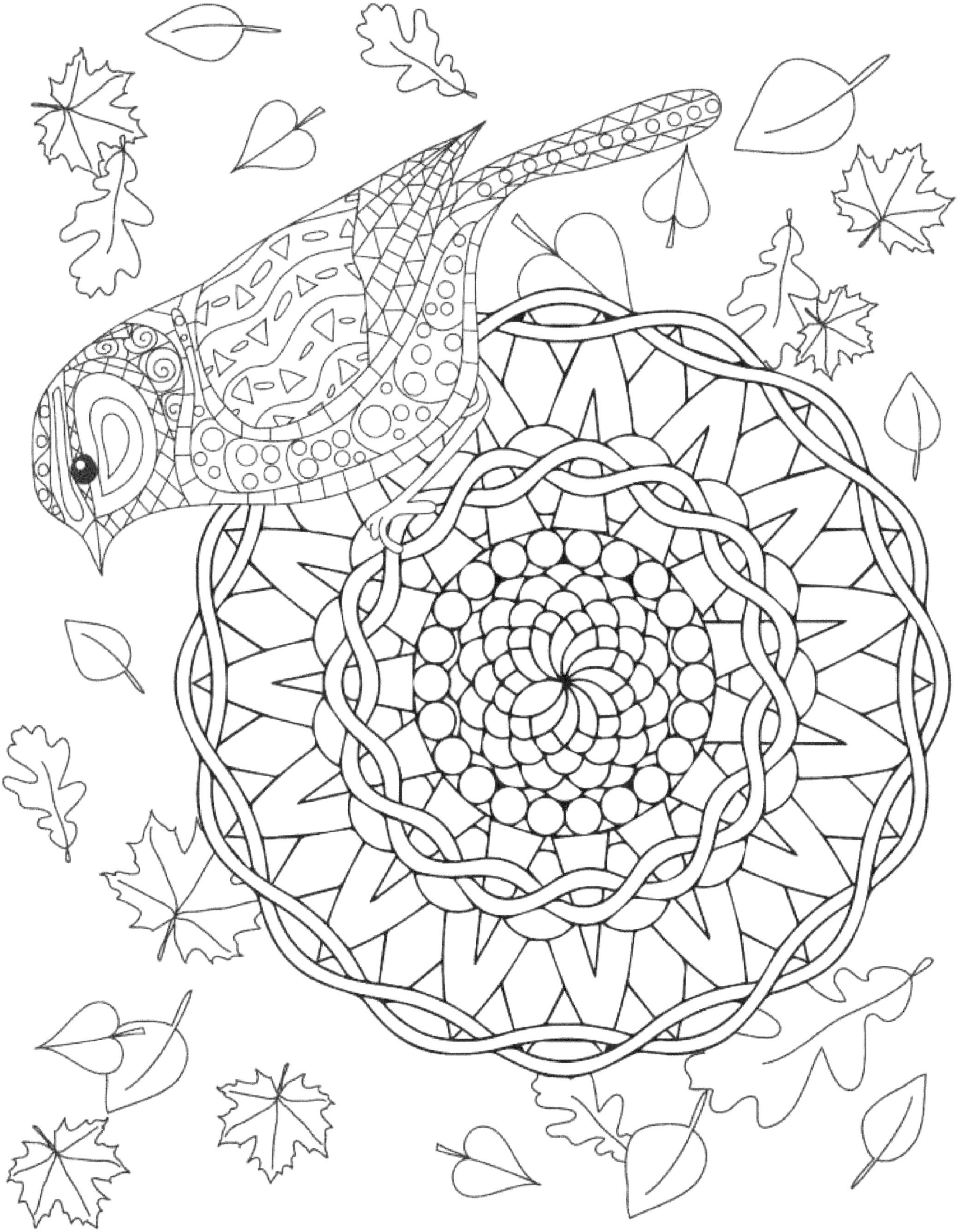

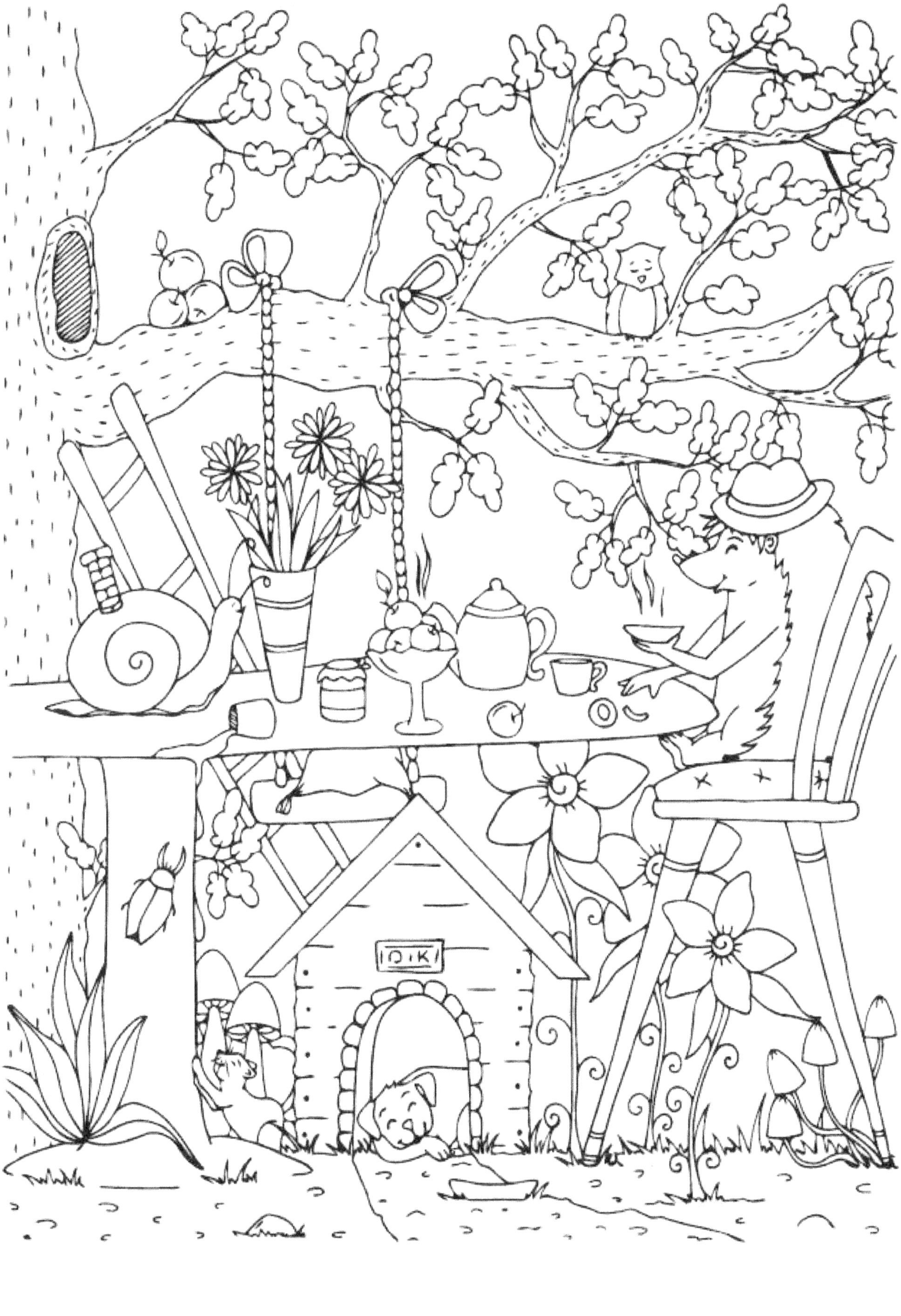

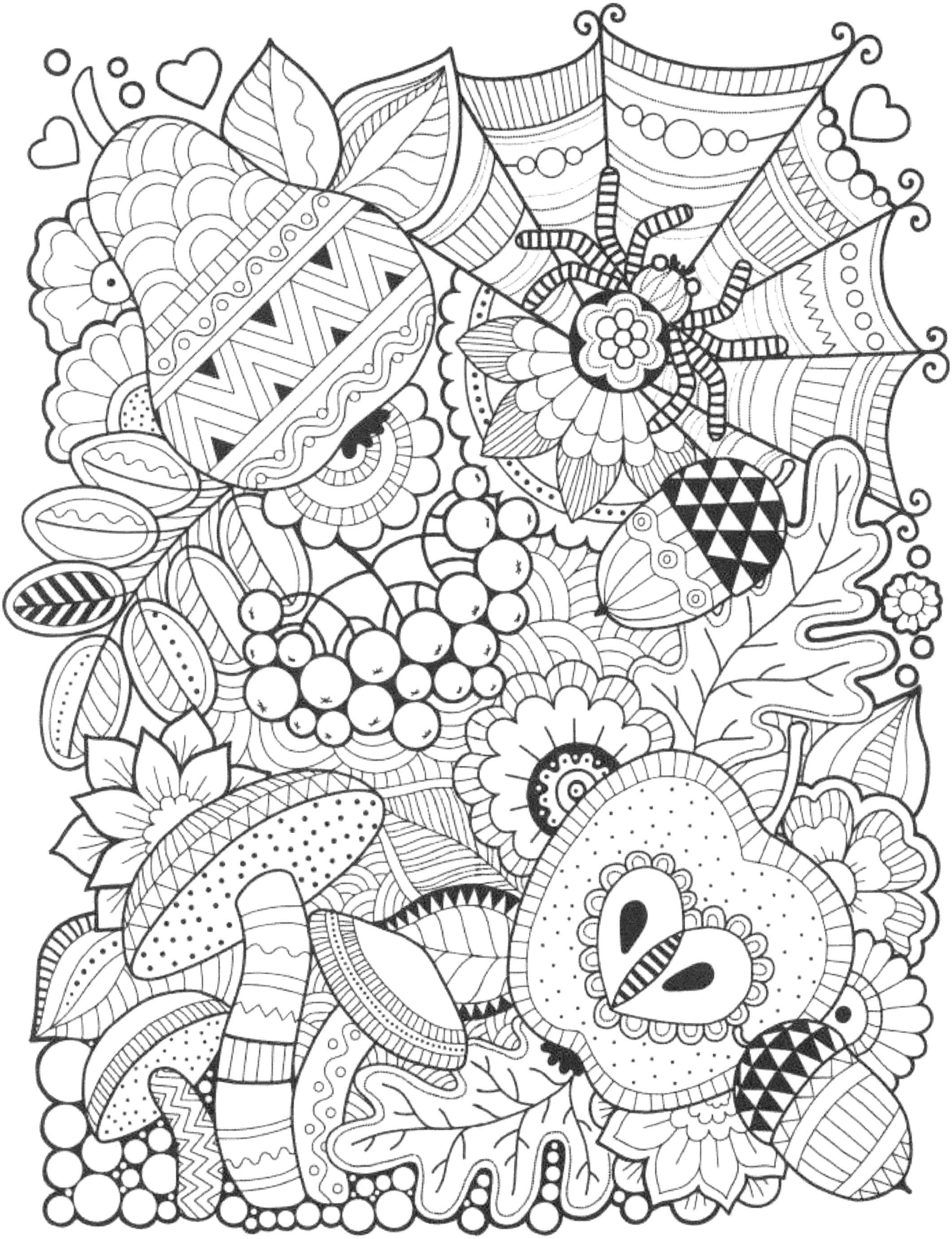

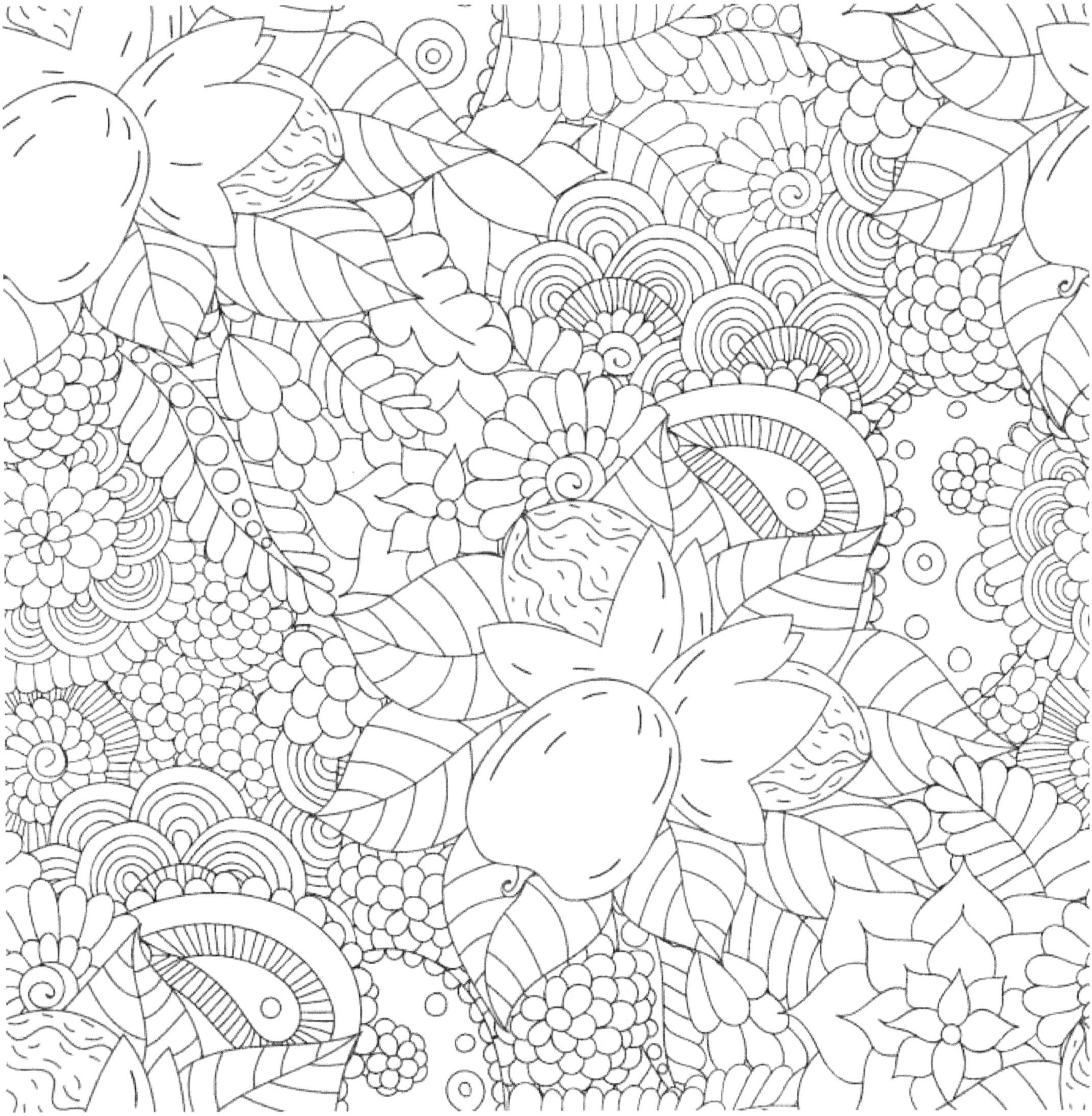

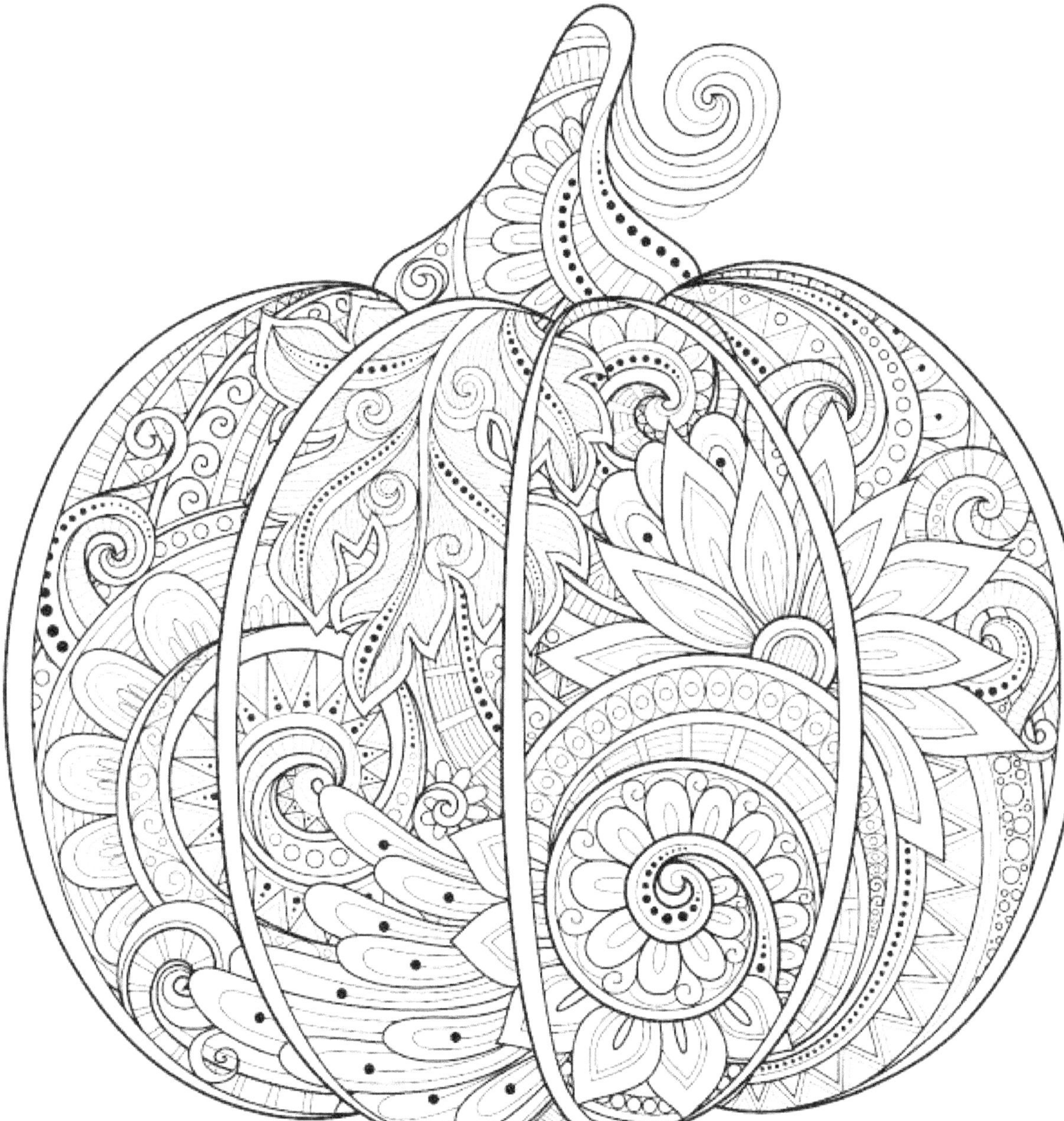

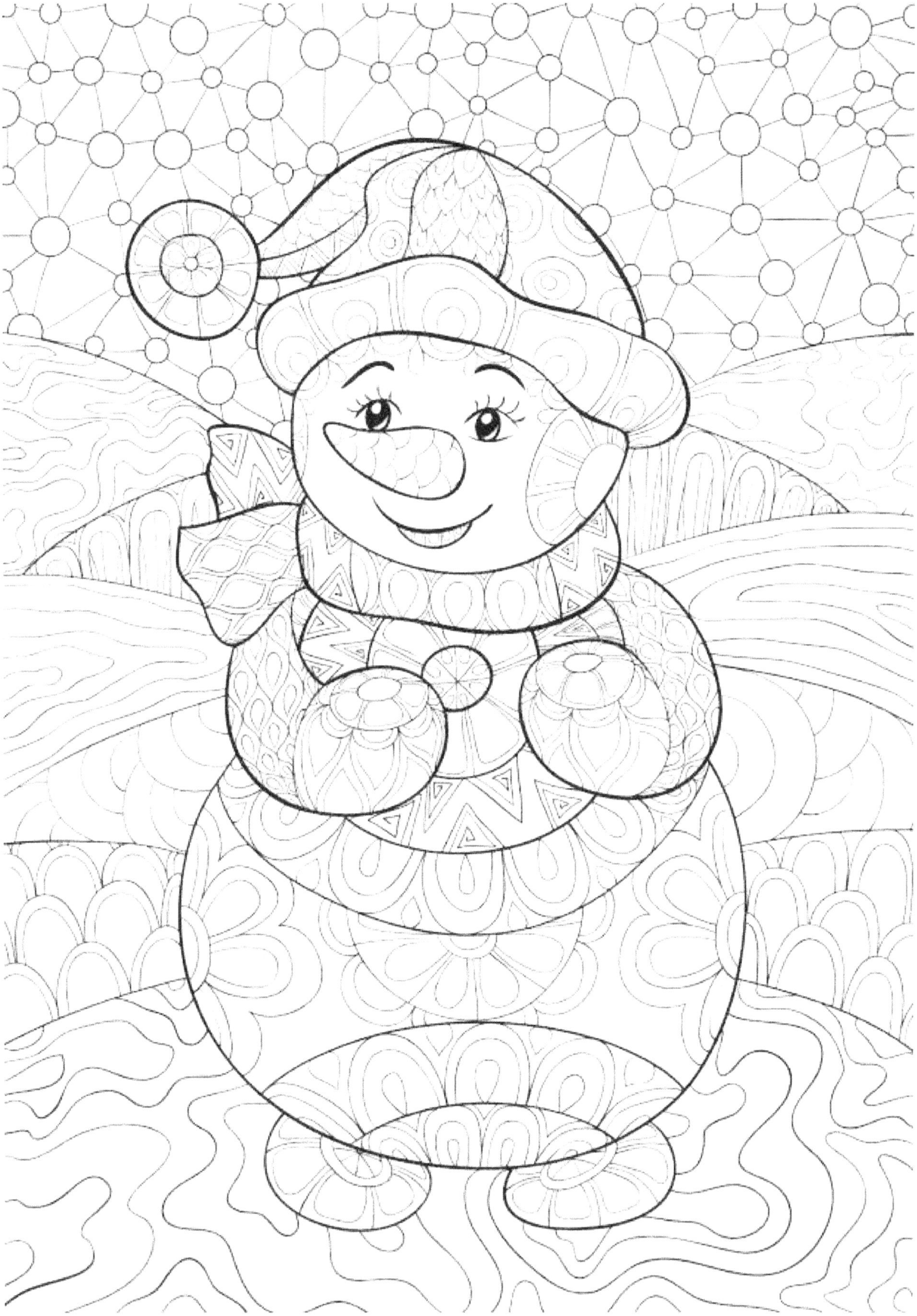

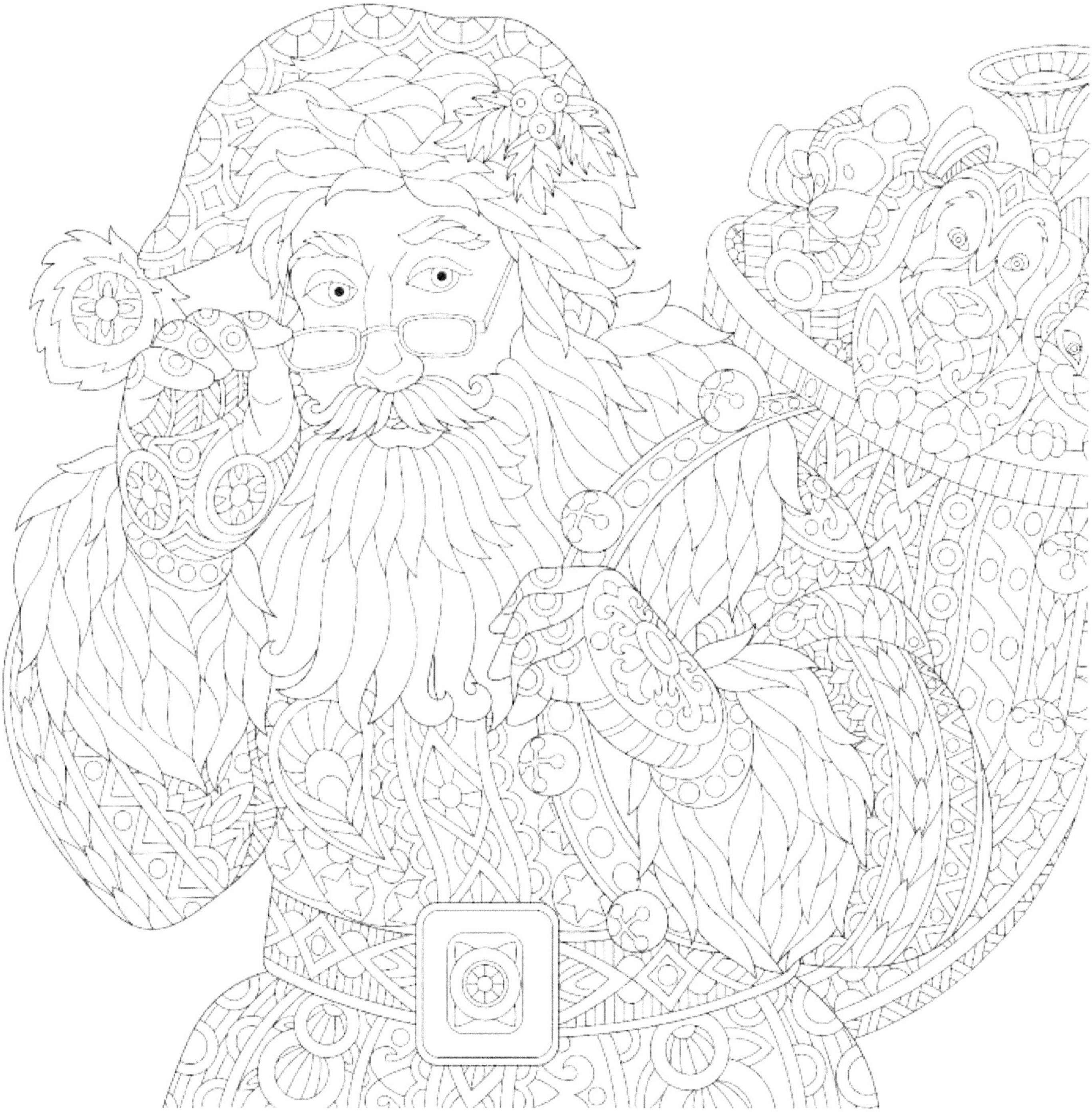

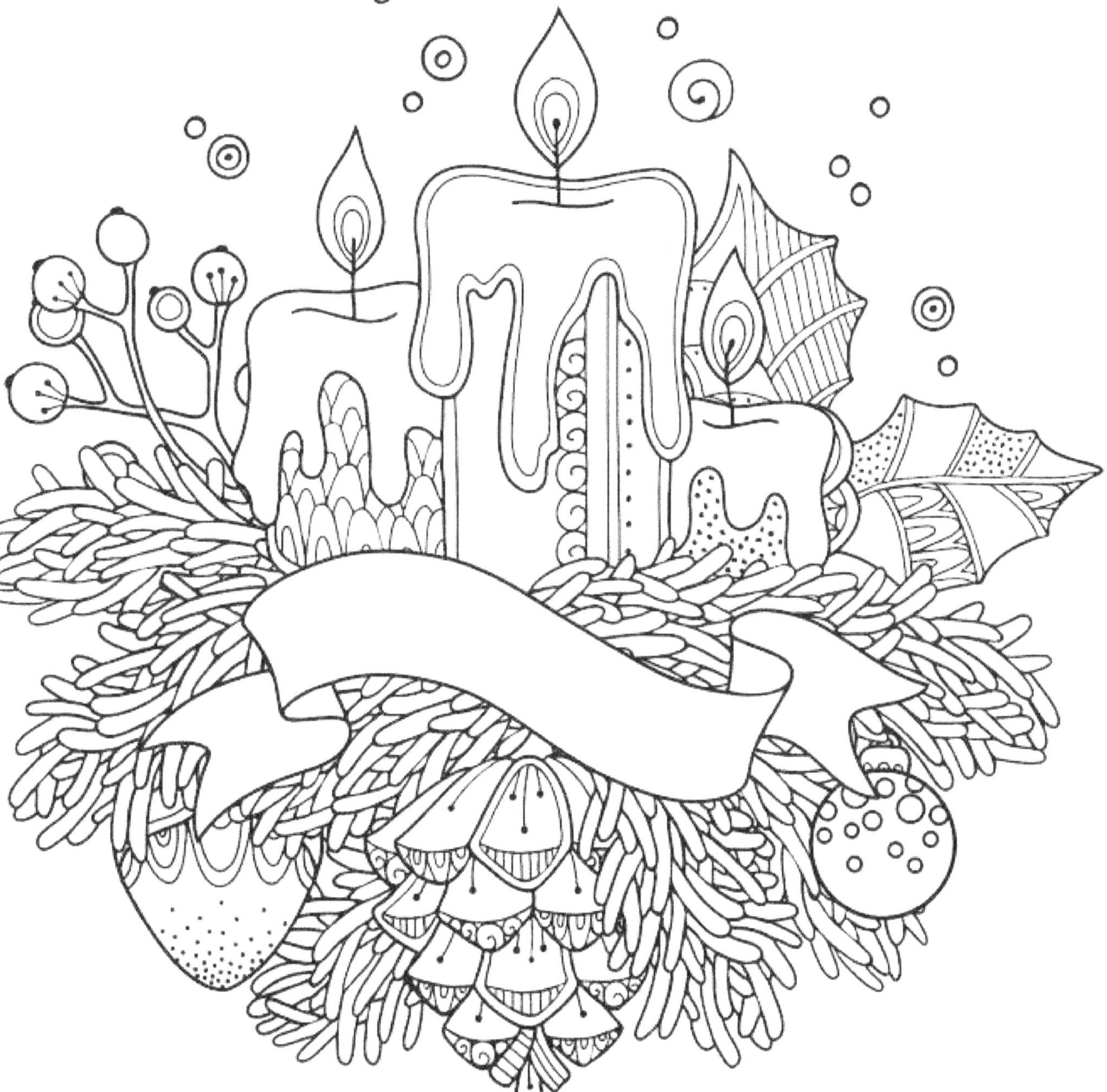

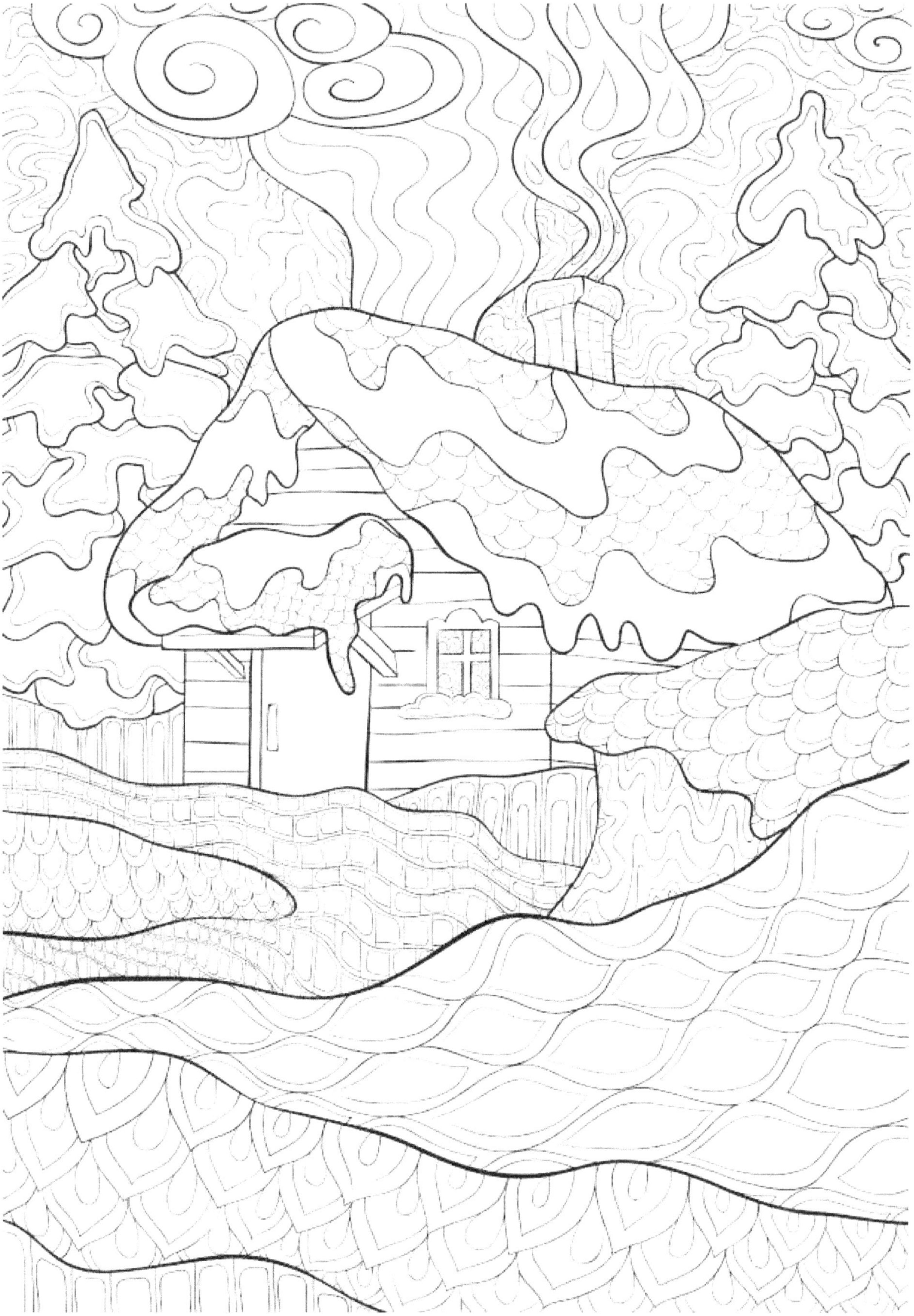

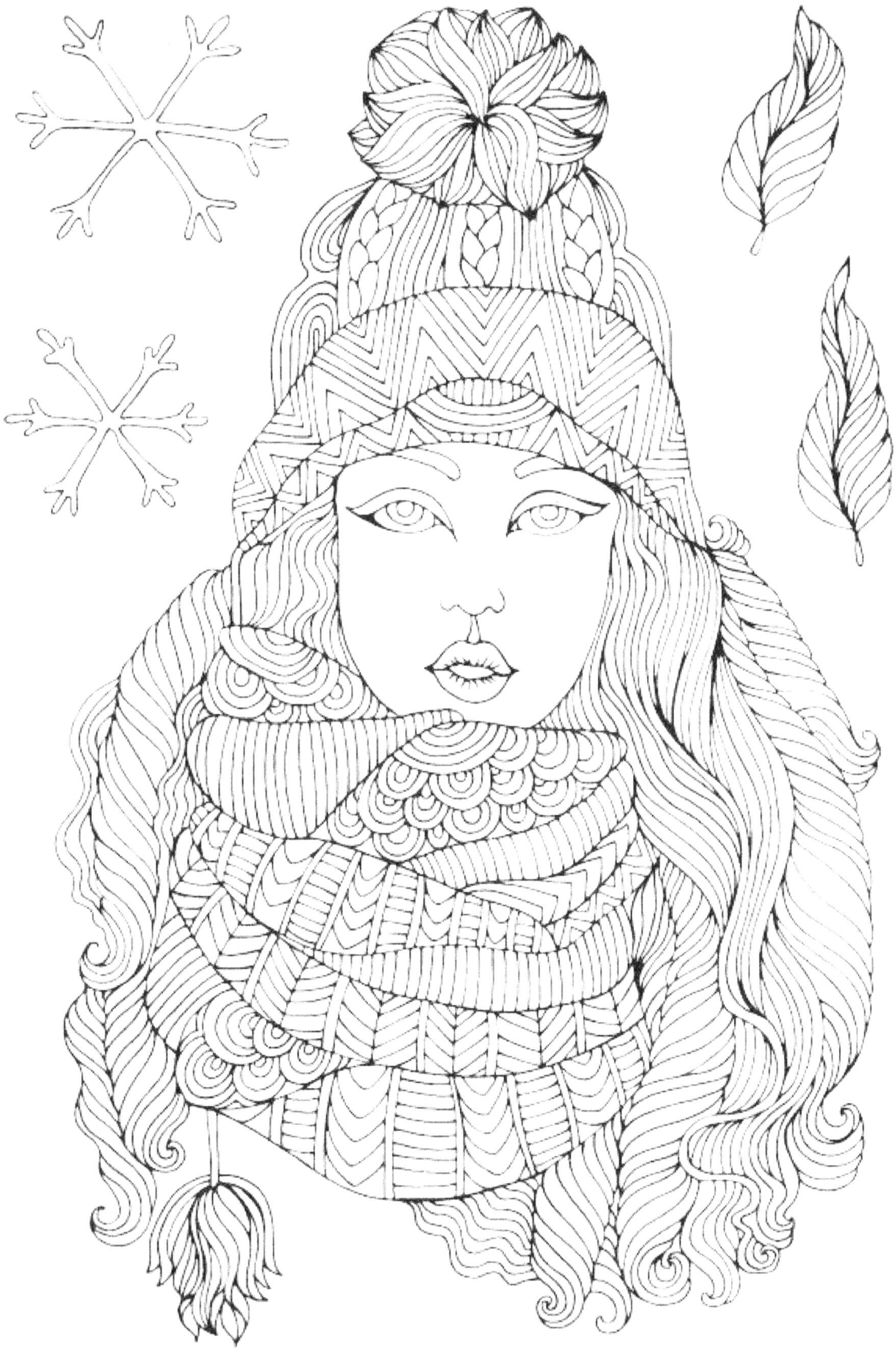

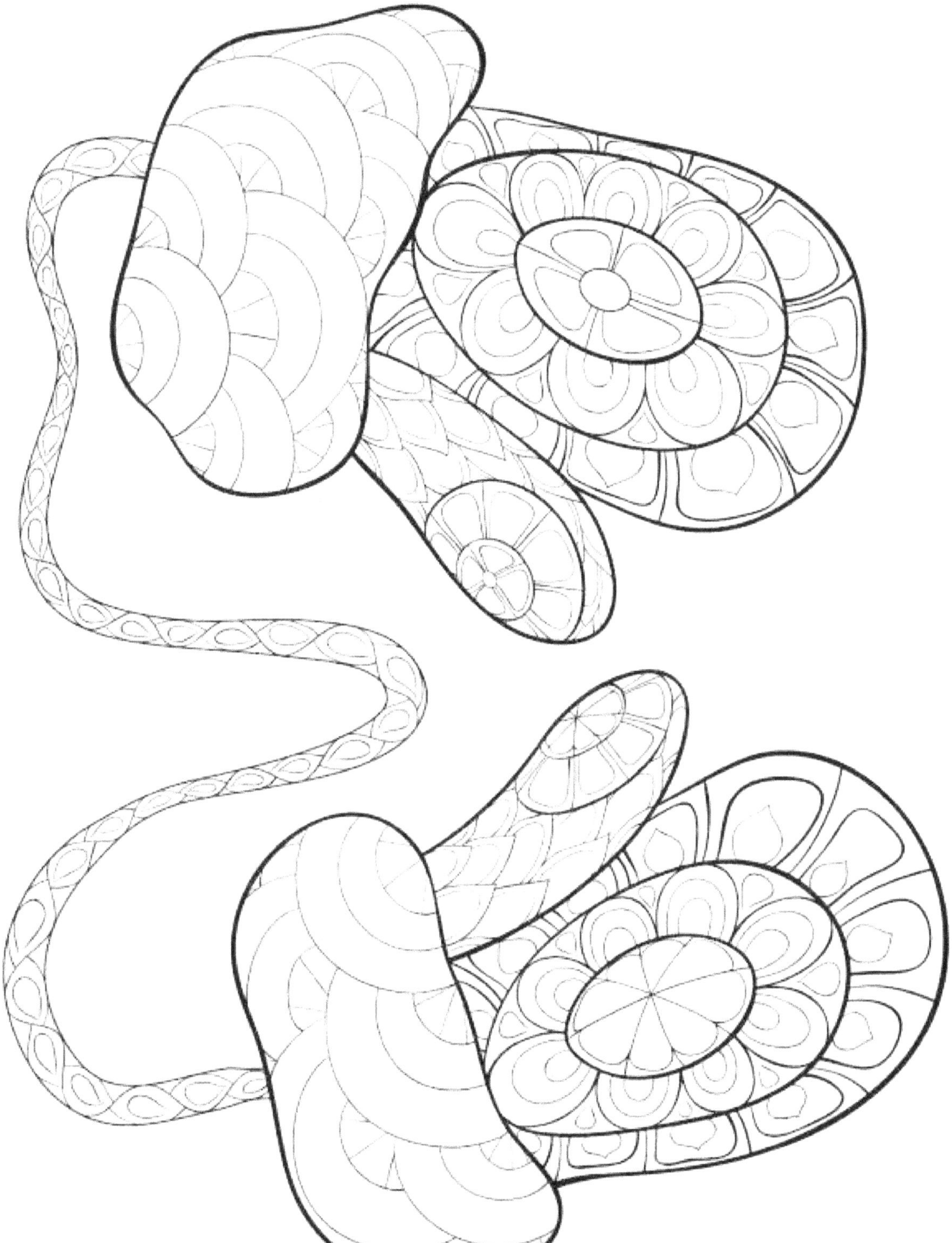

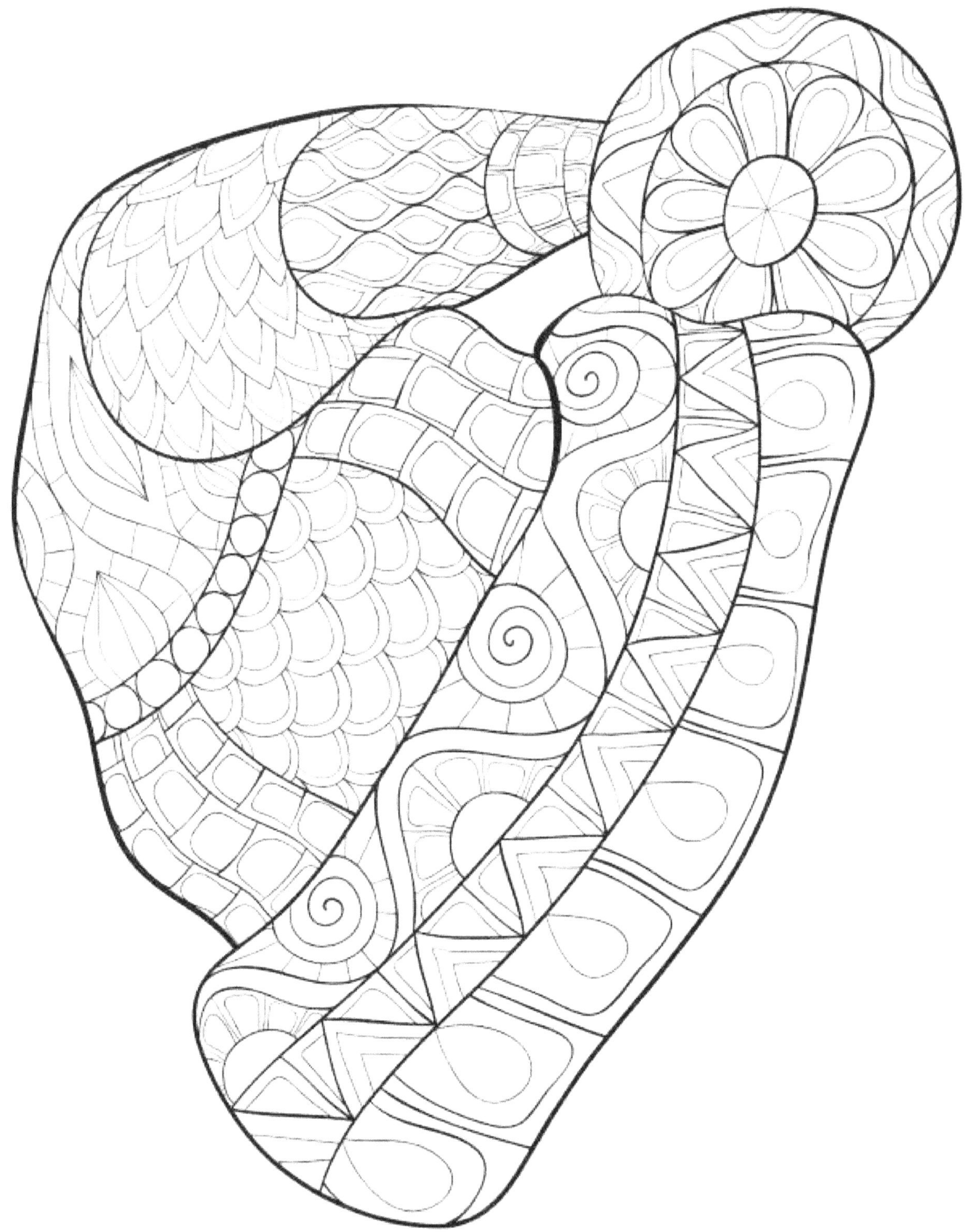

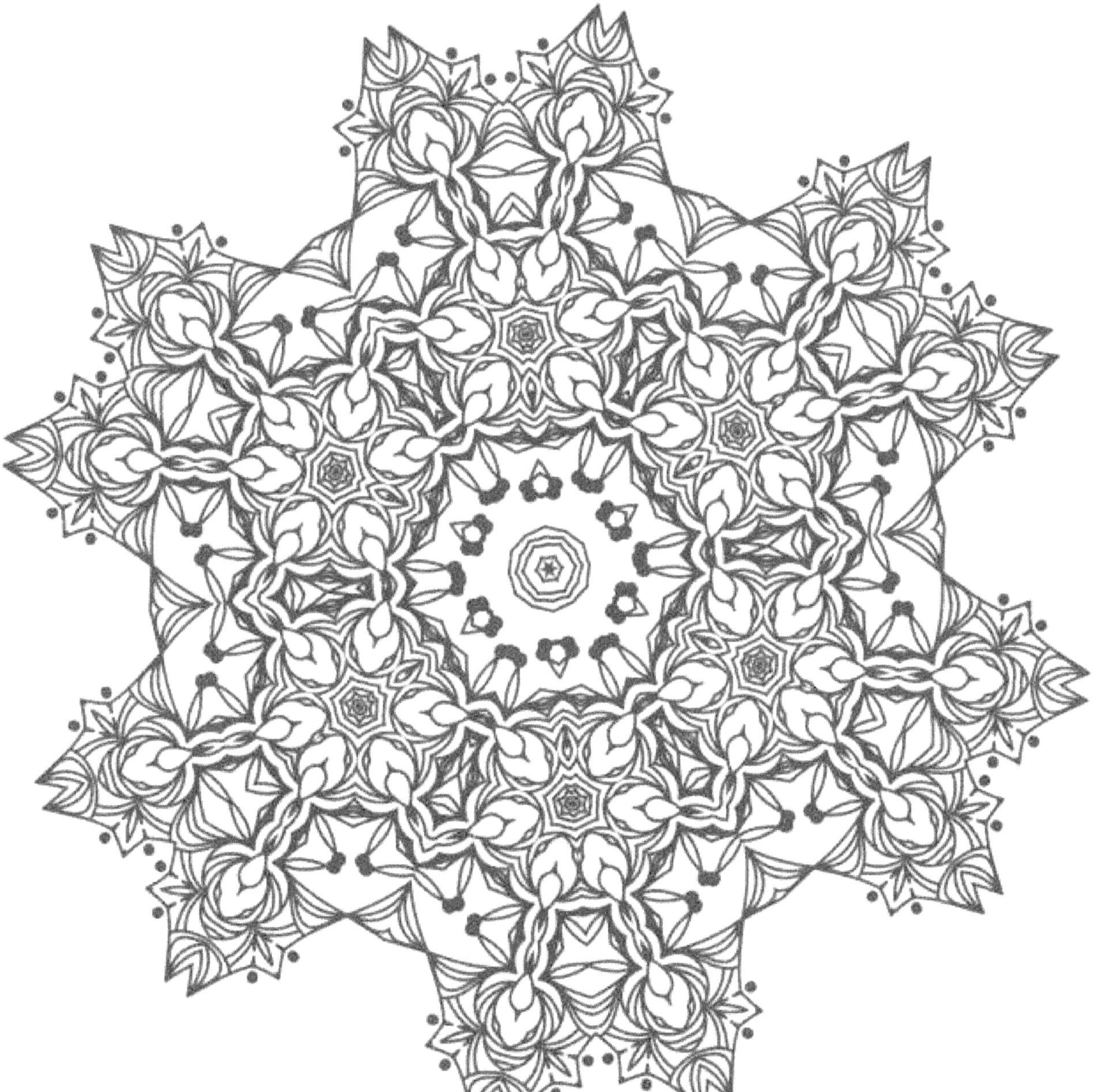

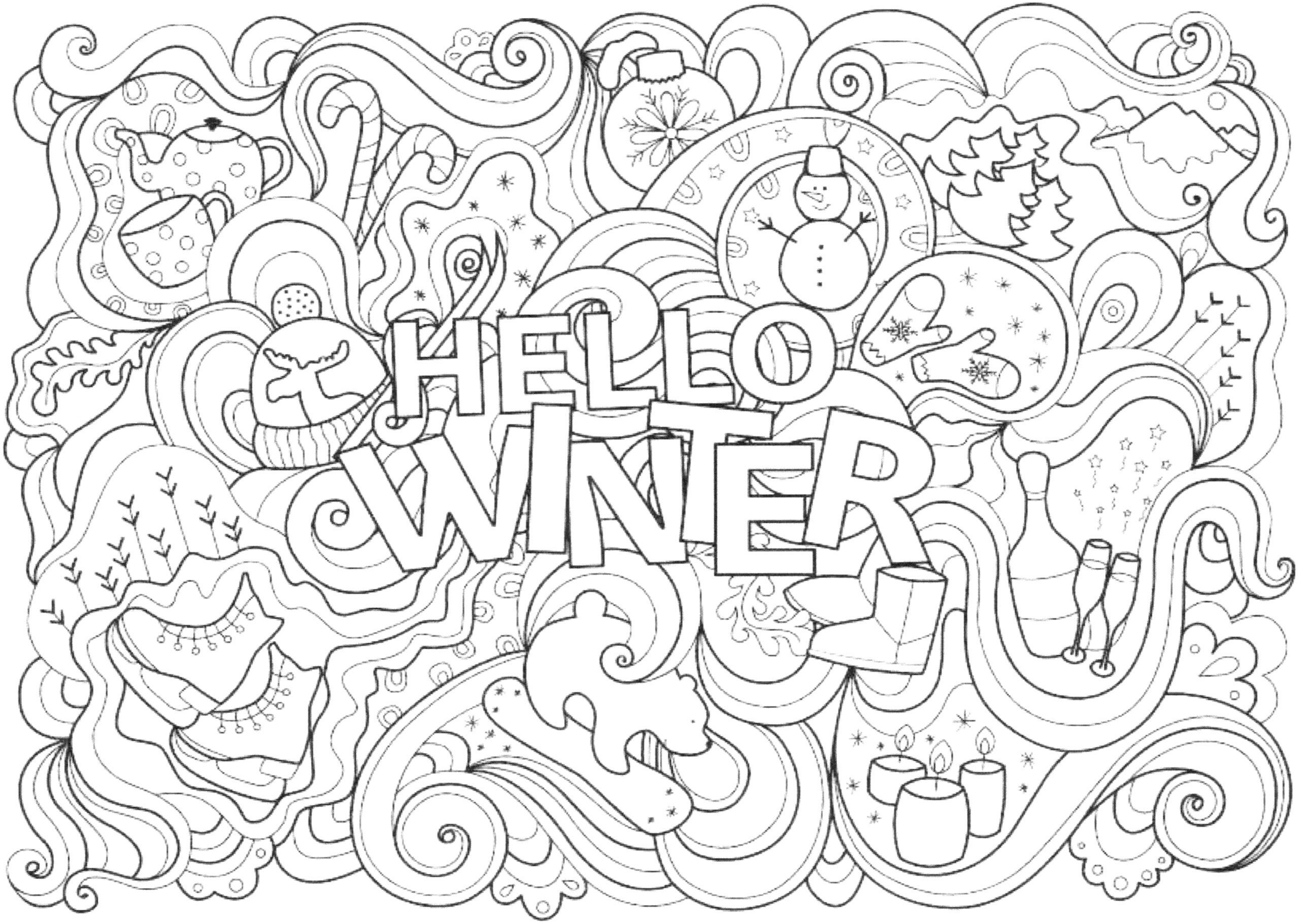
HELLO
WINTER

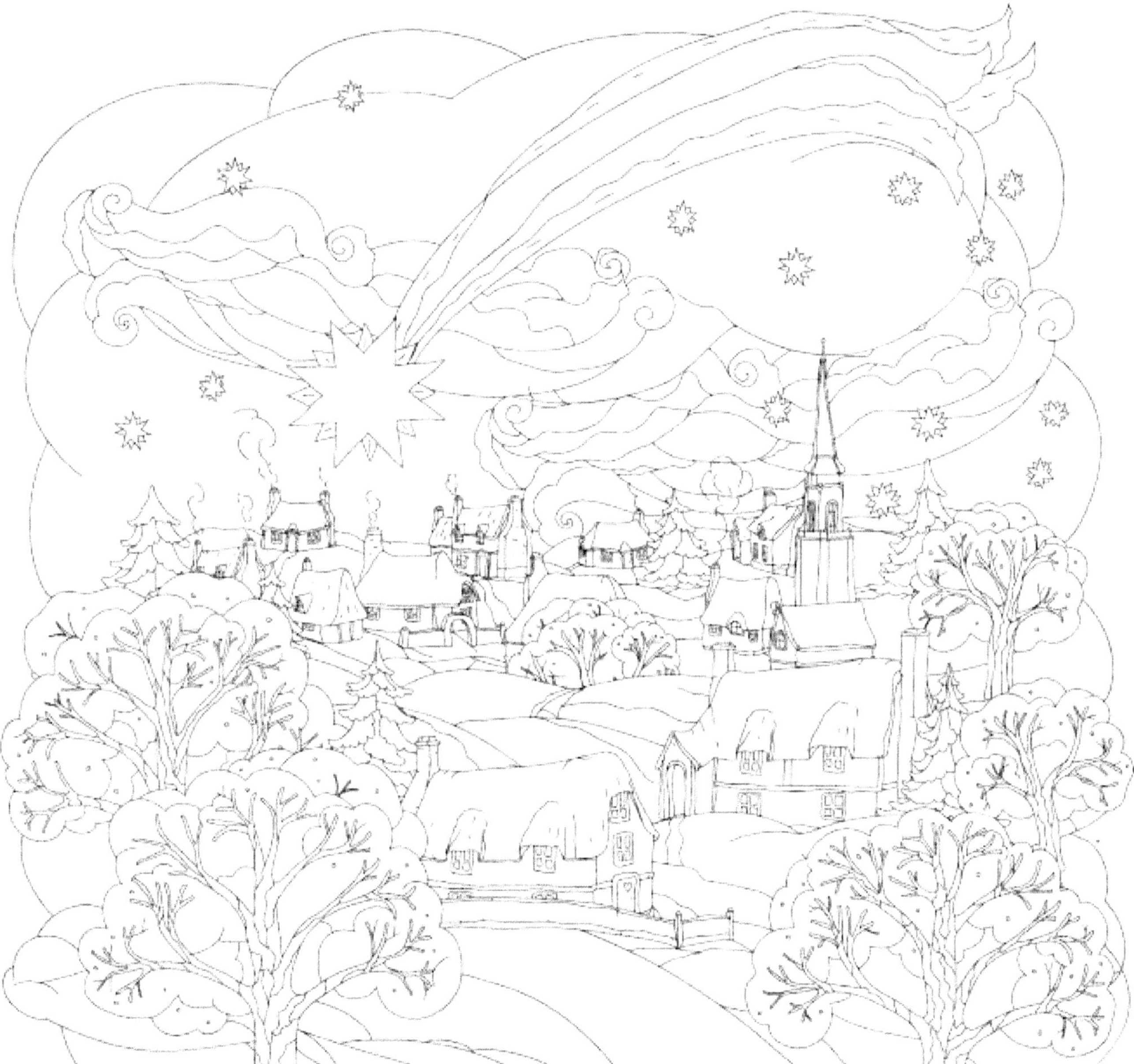

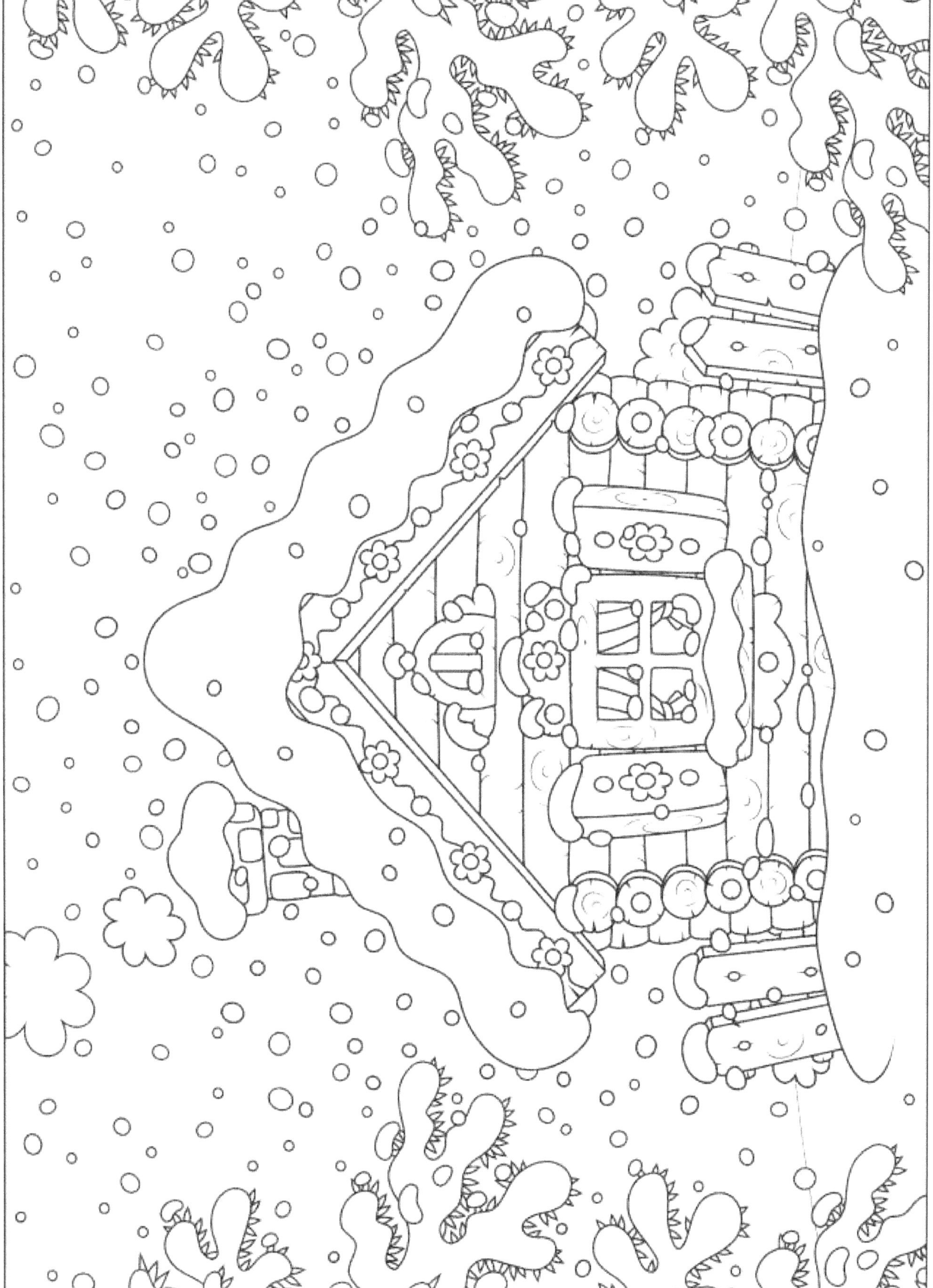

www.ingramcontent.com/pod-product-compliance
Lightning Source LLC
Chambersburg PA
CBHW081015170526
45158CB00010B/3046
9781091427716